This book is presented to:

Deborah and Daniel

on this day of:

_____

by:

Joan and Hua-Wei

THE AMAZING BOOK

Volume I

A Bible Translation for Young Readers

John R. Kohlenberger III
Noel Wescombe

MULTNOMAH

THE AMAZING BOOK, VOLUME 1
© 1991 by John R. Kohlenberger III and Noel Wescombe
Published by Multnomah Press
10209 SE Division Street
Portland, Oregon 97266

Multnomah Press is a ministry of Multnomah School of the Bible,
8435 NE Glisan Street, Portland, Oregon 97220.

Illustrations and design by Brian Ray Davis.
Edited by Al Janssen and Rodney L. Morris.

Permission to use the cartoon characters from "The Amazing Book" videocassette, © 1988 by
Multnomah Productions and The Bridgestone Group, is gratefully acknowledged.

Printed in the United States of America.

Library of Congress Cataloging-in-Publication Data

Kohlenberger, John R.
    The amazing book : a Bible translation for young readers / John R. Kohlenberger, Noel
Wescombe.
      p.   cm.
    Summary: A paraphrase of the Bible in simple language. Includes questions and
definitions of key terms.
    ISBN 0-88070-446-2 (v. 1)
    1. Bible—Paraphrases, English. 2. Bible—Examinations, questions, etc. [1. Bible—
Paraphrases.] I. Wescombe, Noel. II. Title.
BS551.2.K587   1991
220.9'505—dc20   91-16221
                                                        CIP
                                                          AC

91 92 93 94 95 96 97 98 99 00 — 10 9 8 7 6 5 4 3 2 1

Contents

Introduction

How can children learn what the Bible says? Bible storybooks tell children the stories of creation, Moses, David and Goliath, Daniel in the lions' den, and others. But what is God's message behind those stories? How do they fit together as part of God's total plan?

The Amazing Book acquaints beginning Bible readers with key people, events, and ideas of the Bible. It begins with God's creation of heaven and earth. It ends with his creation of the new heaven and the new earth. And in between, Doc Dickory, Revver, and Rikki help its readers discover what God said and did throughout history.

The biblical text of *The Amazing Book* was selected, translated, and organized for young readers. It is designed to be read by children who have mastered the basics of learning to read and are now busy reading to learn. It introduces them to the great God of the universe. Readings focus on major texts that show God's work in his world. Readers learn what God is like, how he has acted throughout biblical history, and how he still works in our lives. Readings are selected from all major types of biblical literature: history and law, poetry and wisdom, Gospel and Acts, letter and prophecy. This gives the young reader more of a balanced diet on the biblical feast; not just a snack on the best-known stories.

The readings are also organized in chronological order. This gives the young reader a sense of the flow of biblical history, and an appreciation of the ongoing revelation of the person of God and his work throughout Bible times. A timeline on page 141 gives approximate dates for key episodes of biblical history.

The Amazing Book is arranged in seventy-two sections or readings. The sections can be read at any pace. However, two readings per week would make the book last for nine months. This would supplement well any Christian school or home school curriculum, or offer a wonderful addition to public school studies. We recommend that parents and young readers prayerfully read each section on their own and then discuss the text and concepts as a part of family discipleship and devotion.

Each reading begins with a paragraph or two designed to help bridge the gap between a child's world and the world of the Bible. Next, selected words are listed and their meaning explained. "In Other Words" not only defines new words, but also provides the young reader with a basic biblical and theological vocabulary. These words are also listed alphabetically in the glossary at the back of *The Amazing Book*. After the introduction and the definitions comes the Bible text: "In God's Words." It is followed by some questions. The questions

Introduction

help readers remember what they have read and put them "In Your Words." Some questions ask for simple answers that can be found right on the page. Other questions make the reader think awhile before they can be answered. Still other questions ask the reader to do things that please God.

John Kohlenberger developed a new translation of selected Bible texts for *The Amazing Book.* The selections are original translations from the Hebrew Old Testament and the Greek New Testament. Words are drawn from the average vocabulary of third and fourth grade. Special biblical and theological terms reflect the consensus of standard English Bibles, such as the New International Version, the New American Standard Bible, the International Children's Bible, and the New Revised Standard Version. Thus *The Amazing Book* is an excellent primer to reading any major Bible translation.

In *The Amazing Book* we chose to render the name of God as Yahweh rather than Lord, as do most other versions. We did this for several reasons. God and Lord are titles of God; labels that are also used by the false gods of the world. Yahweh is God's personal name, unique and shared with no other "god" or created being. Yahweh reveals the God of the Bible as the God who is with his people, who loves them and saves them from their sins and from their distress. Yahweh is also the most common name of God in the Bible, occurring over 6800 times in the Old Testament! It is also built into the name Jesus, which means "Yahweh is salvation." We want young readers—and their parents—to become familiar with this powerful name. We included it throughout the Old Testament readings. We defined it twice (readings 4 and 19). And we showed its amazing significance in the life of Jesus in reading 62.

John and Noel developed *The Amazing Book* because they wanted children to enjoy reading the Bible on their own. Many children have Bible story books full of wonderful pictures and fascinating stories. They love to have their parents read those books to them. Other children have children's Bibles. These children love to carry their Bibles to church and Sunday school. But often they find the text difficult to read and understand. We hope our book with its combination of readable text, exciting pictures, and reading helps will open the world of the Bible to younger readers. And with a little help from Doc and Dewey, Rikki and Revver, children everywhere will succeed when they read the Bible on their own.

1
God Makes the World

Wouldn't it be fun to make something just by saying its name? You could say "bat" and a new baseball bat would land on your floor. Or you could say "teddy" and a teddy bear would peek out from under your covers. Maybe you're hungry. Just say "peanut butter sandwich" and lunch is ready. Your room would be full of all sorts of things! You'd feel strong if you could make things that way. Well that's how God made all things. He said their names and they were made. Our God is very strong!

In Other Words

appear. Now you can see it. Before you could not. It appeared!

empty. Nothing on the earth was like we see it today. There were no apples and no caterpillars. The only thing on the earth was water.

order. When things have order, they are in the right place. And they work just right. God put all things on the earth in the right place and made them work just right.

In God's Words
Genesis 1:1-13

[1]In the beginning God made the heavens and the earth. [2]The earth had no **order** and was **empty**. It was dark all over the deep sea. And the Spirit of God was also over the waters.

[3]Then God said, "Let there be light!" And there was light. [4]God saw that the light was good. God put the light and the darkness in their own places. [5]God called the light "day" and the darkness "night." The night came and then morning came. This was the first day.

[6]Then God said, "Let there be something to put the water in

11

different places." ⁷So God made the air to put the water on the earth in a different place from the water in the sky. So it was that way. ⁸God called the air "sky." The night came and then morning came. This was the second day.

⁹Then God said, "Let the water under the sky be in one place, and let dry ground **appear**." So it was that way. ¹⁰God called the dry ground "land" and the waters "seas." God saw that it was good.

¹¹Then God said, "Let the plants grow on the land. Let some plants and trees make seeds. Let others grow fruit with seeds in it. Let these seeds grow into the same kinds of plants." So it was that way.

¹²The land grew plants. Some plants and trees made seeds. Others made fruit with seeds in it. The seeds grew into the same kinds of plants. God saw that it was good. ¹³The night came and then morning came. This was the third day.

In Your Words

1. God didn't use tools out of a toolbox to make his world. How did he make his world?

2. What do you think water above the sky looked like?

3. God is very strong. He loves you and me. He wants to help us do good things. He is strong enough to help you do good things! What do you want him to help you do?

2
Lights, Plants, and Animals

God didn't want an empty earth. He filled it. God said, "Tame animals." Cows, goats, and sheep appeared. God said, "Wild animals." Out jumped lions and tigers and bears. Oh my!

God didn't want an earth without order. He made day and night. Now the earth had order. It had time. Look out your window. Is the sun just coming up. It's morning. Is the sun high over your head? It's noon. Maybe it's dark. It must be night. God made the sun and moon to give order to our days.

Now the earth will be full. And all things will work just right.

In Other Words

bless. God's blessing is his promise to do something good. He always makes his promises happen.

kinds. Dogs have puppies and cats have kittens. Dogs don't have kittens! And cats don't have puppies! People, animals, and plants always have babies that are like them.

In God's Words

Genesis 1:14-25

[14]Then God said, "Let there be lights in the sky to put the day and the night in their own places. Let these lights show special times and seasons and days and years. [15]Let them shine in the sky to give light on the earth." So it was that way.

[16]God made two big lights. The biggest light shined in the day and the smaller light in the night. He made the stars, too. [17]God put them in the sky to shine on the earth. [18]He made them for the day and the night, and to put light and darkness in their own places.

God saw that it was good. [19]The night came and then morning came. This was the fourth day.

[20]Then God said, "Let the water be filled with living animals. Let birds fly in the sky above the earth." [21]So God made big animals in the sea. He filled the water with all living animals. He made all **kinds** of birds. The sea animals and the birds had babies that were just like them. God saw that it was good.

[22]God **blessed** them and said, "Have many babies and fill the seas. Let the birds have many babies on the land." [23]The night came and then morning came. This was the fifth day.

[24]Then God said, "Let the land be filled with living animals. Let them have babies that are just like them. Let there be tame animals, animals that crawl on the ground, and wild animals. Let them have babies that are just like them." So it was that way.

[25]God made wild animals, tame animals, and all the animals that crawl on the ground. They all had babies that were just like them. God saw that it was good.

In Your Words

1. What did God make on the fifth day?

2. God made order. He made time. Name the four parts of the year he made.

3. God made everything. Do you think that he made you?

3
God Makes Man and Woman

How are people and dinosaurs alike? A dinosaur has eyes. So do I. A dinosaur eats food. So do I. A dinosaur sleeps. And so do I. But I'm not just like a dinosaur! And neither are you. We're made in God's image. People are like animals in some ways. But only people are made in the image of God. That makes us very special.

In Other Words

Holy means different. But it is different God's way. God worked for six days. God rested on the seventh day. The seventh day is different. That is why the seventh day is holy.

image. God made people in his image. That doesn't mean we look like God. It doesn't mean we are as strong as God. And it doesn't mean we are little gods. It means we can talk and think and act like God does.

rest. When we are tired we go to sleep. That's not how God rests. When he rests he's not making any new things.

rule. God wants people to take good care of his world. And he doesn't want anyone to harm his animals just for fun.

In God's Words
Genesis 1:26-2:3

²⁶Then God said, "Let us make man in our **image**, in our likeness. Let them **rule** over the fish of the sea and the birds of the sky. Let them rule over the tame animals, over all the earth, and over all the animals that crawl on the ground."
²⁷So God made man in his own image. He made him in the image of God. He made them male and female. ²⁸God blessed them

and said to them, "Have many babies. Fill the earth and control it. Rule over the fish of the sea, and over the birds of the sky, and over every living animal that crawls on the ground."

²⁹Then God said, "I give you every plant on the whole earth that grows seeds. I give you every tree that grows fruit with seeds in it. They are yours to eat. ³⁰I also give every green plant to all the animals of the earth, to all the birds of the sky, and to all the animals that crawl on the ground. Everything that lives and breathes can eat these plants." So it was that way.

³¹God saw all that he had made. He saw that it was very good. The night came and then morning came. This was the sixth day.

²:¹So the heavens and the earth and all that was in them were finished. ²By the seventh day God had finished his work. So God **rested** from all his work on the seventh day. ³God blessed the seventh day and made it **holy**. He made it holy because he rested on the seventh day from all the work of making the heavens and the earth.

In Your Words

1. Sometimes two words mean the same thing. What word in the reading means the same thing as "image"?

2. How can you take care of five things God has made?

3. If God is resting will he forget about us? How does that make you feel?

4
Adam and Eve in the Garden

Have you ever walked in a garden? Maybe it grew pretty flowers. Maybe it grew squash and carrots and beans. God made a garden too. It was beautiful. It had many trees. He made it for his people. It was the perfect place for them to live. God's garden was called the Garden of Eden. It was near Israel. But it's gone today.

God made the first woman from the first man. He put them together in the garden. God wanted them to be together. He wanted the man and the woman to live there with him forever.

In Other Words

good and **evil**. Good is doing what God wants. Evil is the same as bad. It is the same as wrong. Not doing what God wants you to do is evil.

Yahweh is God's special name. It is a name no one else has. It is a name God gave to himself. His name tells us that he is a God who is always with us and who saves us.

In God's Words
Genesis 2:7-9,15-25

[7]**Yahweh** God made the man out of the dust from the ground. Yahweh God breathed into the man's nose and gave him life. The man became alive.

[8]Yahweh God made a garden in Eden to the east. He put the man in the garden. [9]Yahweh God made all kinds of trees grow out of the ground. The trees were beautiful. Their fruit was good to eat. There were two special trees in the middle of the garden. One was the tree that gives life. The other was the tree that lets people know what is **good** and what is **evil**.

[15]Yahweh God put the man in the Garden of Eden to take care of it and to work there. [16]Yahweh God commanded the man, "You

20

may eat fruit from any tree in the garden. [17]But never eat from the tree that lets people know what is good and what is evil. If you ever eat fruit from that tree you will die!"

[18]Yahweh God said, "It is not good for the man to be alone. I will make him a helper just right for him." [19]Yahweh God had already made all the wild animals and all the birds of the sky. (He had made them from the ground, too.) He brought them to the man to see what names the man would give them. Every living animal got its name from the man. [20]The man gave names to all the tame animals, to the birds of the sky, and to all the wild animals. But none of the animals was the right helper for Adam.

[21]So Yahweh God made the man fall fast asleep. While the man was asleep, Yahweh God took a rib out of the man's side. Then Yahweh God fixed the man's body at the place where he took out the rib. [22]Yahweh God made a woman from the rib he had taken out of the man, and he brought her to the man.

[23]The man said,

"This person's bones came from my bones.
　　Her body came from my body.
Her name is 'woman,'
　　because she was taken out of man."

[24]This is why a man leaves his father and mother and joins his wife when they marry. They become like one person.

[25]The man and his wife were naked. But they were not embarrased.

In Your Words

1. God made two special trees in the middle of the garden. Tell what each tree was like.

2. God tells us things that are right to do. He tells us what things are wrong. Tell five things that you know are right and good. When will you do them this week?

Dewey Bible Facts

In the beginning, the earth had no order and was empty. God took three days to put the world in order. Then in three more days, he filled it!

ORDER		FILLING	
Day 1	God makes light shine in the darkness	Day 4	God fills the sky with lights
Day 2	God makes a place for water in the sky and water on earth	Day 5	God fills the water with animals and the sky with birds
Day 3	God makes dry ground and plants—the first life on earth	Day 6	God fills the land with animals. God makes man and woman to take care of the world

The world is good because God who made it is good!

5
The First Sin

Have you ever heard a snake talk? Eve did. An evil angel made the snake talk. The angel's name is Satan. Some people call him the devil. He hates God. He tells lies. He is not to be trusted.

In Other Words

sin. Remember learning about good and evil? Sin is doing something evil. It is doing something God doesn't want you to do.

smart, **wise**, and **know**. These three words have similar meaning. When good people are smart, they do good things. When evil people are smart, they often do bad things. Smart people know a lot of things. When smart people do good things, that makes them wise.

In God's Words
Genesis 3:1-13

[1]The snake was **smarter** than any of the wild animals Yahweh God had made. He said to the woman, "Did God really tell you not to eat fruit from any tree in the garden?"

[2]The woman said to the snake, "We may eat fruit from the trees in the garden. [3]But God did say, 'Do not eat fruit from the tree that is in the middle of the garden. Do not even touch it, or you will die.' "

[4]The snake said to the woman, "You will not die! [5]God **knows** that if you eat fruit from that tree, you will see new things. You will be like God. You will know what is good and what is evil."

[6]The woman saw that the fruit of the tree was good to eat. She saw that it was beautiful. She wanted the fruit to make her **wise**. So she took some and ate it. She gave some fruit to her husband, and he ate it.

The First Sin

⁷Then they saw new things! They knew they were naked. So they took fig leaves and made some clothes.

⁸Later that day, the man and his wife heard the Yahweh God walking in the garden. They hid from him among the trees. ⁹But Yahweh God called to the man, "Where are you?"

¹⁰The man said, "I heard you in the garden. I was afraid because I was naked, so I hid."

¹¹Yahweh God said, "Who told you that you were naked? Did you eat fruit from the tree? I commanded you not to eat that fruit!"

¹²The man said, "You put a woman here with me. She gave me some fruit from the tree, and I ate it."

¹³So Yahweh God said to the woman, "What have you done?"

The woman said, "The snake tricked me! Then I ate the fruit."

In Your Words

1. Satan is smart. He is strong. But is he as smart as God? Is he as strong as God? How does that make you feel?

2. Why did Adam and Eve hide from Yahweh God? Do you ever try to hide from God when you do bad things? Do you think we can ever hide from God?

3. Eve blamed the snake for her sin. Adam blamed Eve for his sin. Do you blame someone else when you sin? Do you think you can fool God?

4. When we blame someone else, God likes to forgive us. He doesn't like it when we blame others for our sins. What should we do instead of blaming others for our own sins?

6
God Punishes the First Sin

Have you ever ripped your paper when you were trying to erase a mistake? You probably threw it away and started over again. Remember how good everything was when God made the world? He blessed it. Now he is cursing the world he made. He curses Satan. He curses the snake. He even curses the ground. Maybe God should throw his world away and start all over again!

But God made a promise to Eve. He told her that someone from her family would one day crush the snake's head. So God couldn't throw everything away. He had to keep his promise to Eve. He had to let some of her children live to have other children. One day the snake will be crushed. God promised.

In Other Words

curse. When God blesses, he promises to do something good. When God curses, he promises to punish evil or sin.

pregnant. When a woman has a baby growing inside her, she is pregnant.

In God's Words
Genesis 3:14-24

[14]So Yahweh God said to the snake,
"Because you did this,
    I **curse** you!
You are cursed more than all the tame animals
    and all the wild animals!
You will crawl on your belly,
    and you will eat dust all of your life.

26

¹⁵And I will make you and the woman enemies.
  Your children and her children will be enemies.
Her child will crush your head.
  You will bite his heel."

¹⁶Yahweh God said to the woman,
"I will make it very painful when you are **pregnant**.
  When you have children, it will hurt you.
You will want to control your husband.
  But he will rule over you."

¹⁷Yahweh God said to Adam, "You listened to your wife.
  You ate fruit from the tree that I commanded you not to eat.
I curse the ground because of you!
  You will have to work hard for food all of your life.
  When you work, it will hurt you.
¹⁸The ground will grow thorns and weeds.
  You will eat plants from the fields.
¹⁹You will sweat as you work for your food.
  Then you will go back to the ground.
I made you from the ground.
  You are dust, and you will go back to the dust."

²⁰Adam named his wife Eve. He did this because she became the mother of all people who ever lived.
  ²¹Yahweh God made clothes of animal skin for Adam and his wife. He put the clothes on them. ²²Then Yahweh God said, "The man is now like one of us. He knows what is good and what is evil. He must not eat fruit from the tree that gives life. If he does, he will live forever."
  ²³So Yahweh God sent the man out of the Garden of Eden. He made the man work the ground. (The man was made from the ground.) ²⁴Yahweh God sent the man out of the garden. Yahweh God put angels in the Garden of Eden. He put them on the east side. He also put a sword there. The sword looked like fire. It went back and forth to guard the way to the tree that gives life.

In Your Words

1. Do snakes crawl in the dust? Do weeds grow in the dirt? Do mothers hurt when they give birth to their babies? Why do these three things happen?

2. Adam and Eve ate from the tree God told them not to eat from. Since they ate the fruit, what do they know?

3. God punished Adam and Eve. He sent them out of the Garden of Eden. He punished them, but he still cared for them. What did he make for Adam and Eve before he sent them from the garden?

7
Cain and Abel

Things are getting mixed up! God made people to rule the animals. But now the snake is telling Adam and Eve what to do. God made the woman from the man. But now the woman wants to control the man. And God wanted Adam and Eve to live with him in the Garden of Eden forever. But now the man has to work in the dirt outside the garden. Things are so mixed up that one of Eve's boys kills his own brother. Once everything God made was good. Now things don't seem very good.

In Other Words

offering. God owns the whole world. But he still wants us to give some of it back to him. In Bible days, people gave back to God the best of what they worked for.

relations. What a husband and wife do together to make babies.

call on the name of Yahweh. Talking to the right God; praying to God by name.

In God's Words
Genesis 4:1-15, 25-26

¹Adam had **relations** with his wife Eve. She became pregnant and Cain was born. She said, "I have brought forth a man, with Yahweh's help." ²Some time later, Eve had another son named Abel. Abel was Cain's brother.

Abel took care of sheep. Cain was a farmer. ³Some time later, Cain brought an **offering** to Yahweh. He brought some fruit he had grown from the ground. ⁴But Abel brought the best parts of his most valuable sheep. Yahweh accepted Abel and his offering. ⁵But

Cain and Abel

Yahweh did not accept Cain and his offering. So Cain was very angry and looked very sad.

⁶Yahweh asked Cain, "Why are you so angry? Why do you look so sad? ⁷If you do what is good, I will accept you. If you do not do what is good, sin is waiting to get you! Sin wants to control you. But you must rule over sin."

⁸Later, Cain spoke to his brother Abel. They went into the field. There Cain hit his brother Abel and killed him.

⁹Then Yahweh asked Cain, "Where is your brother Abel?"

Cain said, "I don't know. Am I supposed to take care of my brother?"

¹⁰So Yahweh said, "What have you done? Your brother's blood is on the ground! His blood cries out to me like a voice! ¹¹Now you are cursed! You are driven from the ground which soaked up your brother's blood. You killed your brother with your own hands. ¹²You may work the ground. But it will never grow food for you again. You will wander all over the earth."

¹³Cain said to Yahweh, "I can't stand this punishment! ¹⁴Today you are driving me from the ground. I must hide from you. I must wander all over the earth. Whoever finds me will kill me."

¹⁵But Yahweh said to Cain, "That will not happen. If anyone kills Cain, I will punish him seven times worse." Then Yahweh put a mark on Cain. The mark warned anyone who found Cain not to kill him.

²⁵Adam had sexual relations with his wife again. Eve had another son. She named him Seth. She said, "God has granted me another child. He will take Abel's place, since Cain killed Abel." ²⁶Later, Seth had a son. He named him Enosh. At that time people began to **call on the name of Yahweh**.

In Your Words

1. Adam and Eve had two sons. _____ took care of sheep. _____ was a farmer.

2. Is sin waiting to get us just like it was waiting to get Cain? What must we do to prevent sin from getting us?

3. The two brothers gave offerings to God. What will you give back to God?

8
Noah Builds a Boat

Uh oh! Here comes sin again. Now it seems like everybody is bad. People are living like the snake. They are living like Cain. They are hurting each other all the time. Can God find anyone who is good?

There is one good man. His name is Noah. God finds him. God tells Noah to move animals from God's creation into the boat. Can you imagine that? The animals God created were with Noah in the boat! Now Noah and his family will live with the animals just like Adam and Eve did. Noah is going to be busy. He'll have to feed all the animals. He'll have to clean up after all the animals. Do you think he'll ever get any rest?

In Other Words

covenant. If you do something for me, I'll do something for you. Let's write down our promises so we won't forget them. And let's have some other people hear us make our promises to each other. That's a covenant.

righteous. People who are righteous do what is right. They choose to do what God wants them to do.

violence. When there is violence, people are hurting each other. They are attacking each other.

In God's Words
Genesis 6:9-22

[9]This is the story of Noah.

Noah was a **righteous** man. No one could say he did bad things. Noah walked with God. [10]Noah had three sons: Shem, Ham, and Japheth.

32

[11]Everywhere God looked he saw evil. The earth was full of **violence**. [12]God saw how evil the earth was. All the people on earth did evil things. [13]So God said to Noah, "The end of all people is coming! People have filled the earth with violence. So I will destroy these people and the earth with them.

[14]"But you must build yourself a wooden boat. Make rooms in it. Cover it inside and out with pitch. [15]Make it like this. Make the boat 450 feet long, 75 feet wide, and 45 feet high. [16]Make a roof for the boat. Leave a window between the roof and the boat that is 18 inches high. Put a door in the side of the boat. Make lower, middle, and upper floors.

[17]"I am going to bring a flood of water on the earth. I will destroy everything that lives and breathes. I will destroy every man and animal under the sky. Everything on earth will die. [18]But I will make my **covenant** with you. You and your sons, your wife and your

sons' wives will go into the boat. [19]You must also bring into the boat two of every living animal. Keep them alive with you. Bring a male and a female of every animal. [20]Every kind of bird and animal and everything that crawls on the ground will come to you. Keep them alive. [21]You must also take every kind of food that you and the animals eat. Keep it in the boat as food for you and the animals."

[22]Noah did everything the way God commanded him.

In Your Words

1. Draw a picture of Noah's big boat.

2. Noah had a big job. He did his job well. Do you do your jobs well? How can you care for the animals at your house? How can you help keep your house clean?

3. Noah walked with God. That means he did what God wanted him to do. Do you walk with God? What have you done today that shows others you walk with God?

9
After the Flood

Have you ever been caught in the rain? You probably got soaked. If it wasn't too cold, you probably had fun. Imagine being caught in the rain for forty days. How terrible it must have been to be out in the rain for forty nights! The bad people who were living like the snake (remember reading 5?) drowned in the terrible flood. The bad people who were hurting each other all of the time died in the water. Only Noah and his family lived. Only the animals on the boat lived. Aren't you glad God promised never to do this again?

In Other Words

God remembers. When you remember something, it means you forgot it first. When God remembers something, he's doing what he once promised to do. God never forgets his promises.

In God's Words
Genesis 8:1-14

[1]**God remembered** Noah, and all the wild animals, and all the tame animals in the boat. God sent a wind to blow over the earth. The flood water went down. [2]The springs in the deep sea stopped pouring out water. The clouds in the sky stopped pouring down floods of rain. [3]The flood water on the earth kept going down. The water went down for one hundred and fifty days. [4]On the seventeenth day of the seventh month, the boat landed on the mountains of Ararat. [5]The water kept going down until the tenth month. On the first day of the tenth month, they could see the tops of the mountains.

[6]After forty days, Noah opened the window he had made in the boat. [7]He sent out a raven. It flew back and forth until the water had dried up from the earth. [8]Then Noah sent out a dove to see if the water that covered the ground was gone. [9]The dove could find no

place to land. Water still covered all of the earth. So the dove came back to the boat. Noah reached out his hand and took the dove. He brought it back inside the boat.

[10]Noah waited seven more days. Once again he sent out the dove from the boat. [11]The dove came back to him in the evening. In its beak was a fresh olive leaf! Then Noah knew the water that covered the earth was gone. [12]Noah waited seven more days. He sent the dove out again. But this time it did not come back.

[13]It was the first day of the first month of the year Noah turned 601. The water had dried up from the earth. Noah removed the covering from the boat. He saw that the ground was dry. [14]By the twenty-seventh day of the second month the earth was completely dry.

In Your Words

1. Why didn't the dove come back the last time Noah sent it out?

2. Tell what you think happened when the animals finally got out of the boat. Where did they go? What did they do?

3. Dry ground! God remembered his promise. Noah and his family are still alive. Tell a promise God has made to you. Will he remember?

10
God's Promise to Noah

When was the last time you saw a rainbow? Did it make you think about God's promise not to flood the earth? Did you think of it as God's covenant written in the sky?

Just think how Noah felt when he saw a rainbow. He probably got a little nervous whenever he felt a raindrop. When he saw the dark rain clouds coming, he probably remembered the terrible flood. But when he saw God's rainbow, I'm sure he was glad. One wild boat trip was enough for the good man, Noah.

In Other Words

altar. A pile of stones. People made their offerings to God on an altar.

clean animals and **clean birds**. These are animals God wanted to be given back to him as offerings.

In God's Words
Genesis 8:15-9:11

[15]God said to Noah, [16]"Come out of the boat. You and your wife, your sons and their wives, come out. [17]Bring out every living thing that is with you. Bring out the birds, the animals, and all the animals that crawl on the ground. They must once again swarm all over the earth. They must have many babies on the earth."

[18]So Noah came out with his sons and his wife and his sons' wives. [19]All the living things came out of the boat. All the animals that crawl, all the birds, everything that moves on the earth came out. They came out by families.

[20]Then Noah built an **altar** to Yahweh. He took some of all the **clean animals** and **clean birds**. He burned them as offerings on the altar. [21]Yahweh was pleased with the sweet smell of the offerings. He said to himself, "Never again will I curse the ground because of people. Their thoughts are evil from the time they are children. Never again will I destroy all living things, as I just did.

[22]"As long as the earth is here,
    there will be planting and harvest.
Cold and heat,
    summer and winter,
day and night
    will never stop."

[9:1]God blessed Noah and his sons. He said to them, "Have many children and fill the earth. [2]All the animals of the earth and all the birds of the air will fear you and be afraid of you. Every animal that crawls on the ground and all the fish of the sea will fear you. I give them to you. ³Everything that lives and moves will be food for you. I already gave you green plants to eat. Now I give you everything to eat.

⁴"But you must not eat meat that still has its 'life' (its blood) in it. ⁵I will require your death if you kill someone. If an animal kills a person, I will require its death. If a person kills another person, I will require his death.

⁶"Whoever kills a person,
  must be killed by another person.
For God made people in the image of God.

⁷"You must have many children. Fill the earth with many, many people."

⁸Then God said to Noah and to his sons, ⁹"I am making my covenant with you and with your family after you. ¹⁰My covenant is with every living thing that was with you. It is with the birds, the tame animals, and all the wild animals. It is with all those that came out of the boat with you. It is with every living thing on earth. ¹¹I am making my covenant with you. Never again will the waters of a flood destroy all life. Never again will a flood destroy the earth."

In Your Words

1. Now the animals who once lived with Noah and his family are going to be food for Noah's family! But God made a rule about eating animals. What was the rule God made?

2. Why are wild birds and wild animals afraid of people? Were the birds and animals afraid of Noah on the boat?

3. Will a flood ever again destroy the whole earth? Why?

Babel and Abram

Not sin and punishment again! The people are trying to be gods. They are building a tall tower for their own thrones. Won't they ever learn that Yahweh is God? He will have to punish them again.

Listen to this! *Tov. Agathos. Bonus.* Sounds confusing doesn't it? God punished the people. He made different people speak different languages. They couldn't understand each other any more. *Tov. Agathos. Bonus.* Do you understand these words yet? All that God made was good. But people are not acting good. Along came Abraham. Finally, blessing not cursing. God wants to bless the whole world through Abraham. *Tov. Agathos. Bonus.* Now do you understand these words? They all mean good!

In God's Words

Genesis 11:1-8

[1]The whole world used to have only one language. Everyone spoke the same way. [2]People moved to the east. They found a place to live in Babylon.

[3]They said to each other, "Let's make bricks and bake them until they are hard." They used brick instead of stone, and tar instead of

mortar to hold the bricks together. ⁴They said, "Let us build ourselves a city. Let's build a tower that reaches to the sky. We can make ourselves famous. If we do these things, we will not be scattered over the whole earth."

⁵Yahweh came down to see the city and the tower that the people were building. ⁶Yahweh said, "These people are together. They all speak the same language. This is only the start of what they can do! They can do anything they plan. ⁷So let us go down and confuse their language. Then they will not understand each other."

⁸So Yahweh scattered them from there over the whole earth. They stopped building the city.

Genesis 12:1-7

¹Yahweh said to Abram, "Leave your country. Leave your people and your father's family. Go to the land I will show you.

²"I will make you into a great nation.
  I will bless you.
I will make you very famous,
  you will be a blessing to others.
³I will bless those who bless you,
  I will curse anyone who curses you;
All people on earth
  will be blessed through you."

[4]So Abram left, just as Yahweh told him. Lot went with him. Abram was seventy-five years old when he left Haran. [5]Abram took his wife Sarai and his nephew Lot with him. He took everything they owned, and all the servants they got in Haran. They left for the land of Canaan. Finally they arrived there. [6]Abram walked through the land as far as Shechem. The great tree of Moreh was there. The Canaanites were also in the land.

[7]Yahweh appeared to Abram. He said, "I will give this land to your children who come after you." So Abram built an altar there to Yahweh, who had appeared to him.

In Your Words

1. Why did the people want to build the tall tower?

2. What would you do if you suddenly landed in Germany? Would you try to find other people who spoke English? What do you think the people did when they were scattered?

3. What is God going to give to Abram?

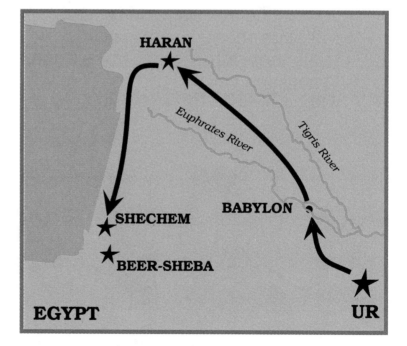

42

12
God Tests Abraham

Have you ever tried counting the stars in the sky? It's fun. At least it's fun for a while. But you'll never be able to count all of the stars. Yes, Abraham knew that! So what did he think when God told him he would have more **descendants** than there are stars in the sky? I'm sure he was surprised. He was most surprised because he and his wife didn't have even one child! How could he have so many descendants when he didn't have any children? God promised to give him a boy. Abraham waited. And he waited. Twenty-five years Abraham waited. Then God gave him Isaac, a son. Now God's asking Abraham to sacrifice his only son. Can you believe it? Will Abraham do it?

In Other Words

descendant. You are a descendant of your parents. That means you came from them. You are a descendant of your grandparents. You are even a descendant of Adam and Eve.

fear God. When bad people fear God, they are afraid of him. When good people fear God, they respect him, they love him, and they obey him.

God knows. Sometimes God says he now knows something. He doesn't mean he has just learned something new. God knows everything. When God says he now knows something he means he has experienced something with us.

worship. When we worship God, we do things that show that we know he is God. We pray to him. We sing to him. We give him our offerings. We are happy that he is our God.

43

In God's Words
Genesis 22:1-18

¹Many years later God gave Abraham a test. God said to him, "Abraham!"

"Here I am," answered Abraham.

²God said, "Take your son and go to the land of Moriah. Yes, take Isaac, your only son, the son you love. Kill him there and burn him as an offering. Do this on the mountain I will tell you about."

³Abraham got up early the next morning. He put a saddle on his donkey. He took two of his servants. Yes, he took his son Isaac. He cut wood for the burnt offering. Then he started to go to the place God had told him about. ⁴Three days later, Abraham saw the place far away. ⁵He said to his servants, "Stay here with the donkey. I and the boy will go over there. We will **worship** God. Then we will come back to you."

⁶Abraham took the wood for the burnt offering. He had his son Isaac carry the wood. Abraham carried a pot with fire in it and a knife. The two of them went on together. ⁷Isaac said to his father, Abraham, "Father?"

"Yes, my son?" answered Abraham.

Isaac said, "I see fire and I see wood. But where is the lamb we will burn as the offering?"

⁸Abraham answered, "God himself will provide the lamb for the burnt offering, my son." The two of them went on together.

⁹They reached the place God had told Abraham about. Abraham built an altar there. He put the wood on it. Then he tied up his son Isaac! He put him on the altar, on top of the wood. ¹⁰Abraham reached out his hand. He took the knife to kill his son! ¹¹But the angel of Yahweh shouted to him from heaven, "Abraham! Abraham!"

"Here I am," answered Abraham.

¹²The angel said, "Do not lay a hand on the boy! Do not do anything to him! Now **I know** that you **fear God**. I know because you did not keep your only son from me."

¹³Abraham looked up. There he saw a ram. Its horns were

44

caught in a bush. He went over and took the ram. He killed the ram and burned it as an offering instead of his son. [14]So Abraham called that place "Yahweh Provides." And to this day people say, "On the mountain of Yahweh, Yahweh Provides."

[15]The angel of Yahweh called to Abraham from heaven a second time. [16]He said, "This is what Yahweh says: 'Because you did not keep your only son from me, I make you a promise. [17]I promise to bless you. I promise to give you as many children as the stars in the sky and as the sand on the seashore. Your children will conquer the cities of their enemies. [18]Through your children all people on earth will be blessed. I promise this because you obeyed me.' "

In Your Words

1. God knows everything. He knew Abraham would obey him. So why did God test Abraham?

2. What did God give Abraham so he would not have to sacrifice his son Isaac? Who has God given to us so we won't have to die for our sins?

3. Isn't it good to read about someone who does what God wants him to do? Abraham trusts God. What do you want to trust God to do for you?

13
Joseph's Amazing Dreams

What happens when you fall asleep? When Adam fell asleep, God made Eve from his rib! When Joseph fell asleep, God spoke to him in his dreams! Sometimes I dream too. But my dreams aren't anything like Joseph's dreams. Have the sun, moon, and stars ever bowed down to you in a dream? They haven't in my dreams. Sometimes our dreams can be funny. At other times our dreams can be scary. But Joseph's dreams were special. God told him secret messages in his dreams. From now on people will be calling Joseph "the dreamer." And, oh, what a dreamer he was! (To see how Joeseph fit into Abraham's family, see page 48.)

In Other Words

dream. In the Bible God used dreams to tell special people about secret things he wanted them to know. The most famous people who had these types of dreams were called *prophets*.

In God's Words
Genesis 37:2b-17

[2]Joseph was seventeen years old. This young man and his brothers took care of sheep. His brothers were the sons of Bilhah and Zilpah, his father's wives. Joseph told their father Israel bad things about his brothers.

[3]Joseph had been born when Israel was old. So Israel loved Joseph more than any of his other sons. He made a very special robe for Joseph. [4]Joseph's brothers saw that their father loved him more than any of them. They hated Joseph. They could not say anything nice to him.

[5]Joseph had a **dream**. He told it to his brothers. Then they hated him even more! [6]He said to them, "Listen to this dream I had. [7]We were out in the field tying bunches of grain together. Suddenly my bunch stood up! Your bunches made a circle around mine and bowed down to it."

[8]His brothers said to him, "Do you think this means you will be our king? Do you think you will rule over us?" They hated him even

more because of his dreams and the things he said.

[9]Joseph had another dream. He told it to his brothers. He said, "Look! I had another dream. The sun and the moon and eleven stars bowed down to me."

[10]Joseph told his father and his brothers. But his father scolded him. He said, "What is this dream you had? Do you think this means your mother and I and your brothers will come and bow down to you?" [11]His brothers were jealous of him. But his father kept thinking about these things.

[12]Some time later Joseph's brothers went to Shechem. They took their father's sheep to feed them there. [13]Israel said to Joseph, "Your brothers are feeding the sheep near Shechem. Go there. I am sending you to them."

"I will go," said Joseph.

[14]Israel said to him, "Go and see if your brothers and the sheep are safe. Then come back and tell me." Israel sent him from the Valley of Hebron. So Joseph went to Shechem.

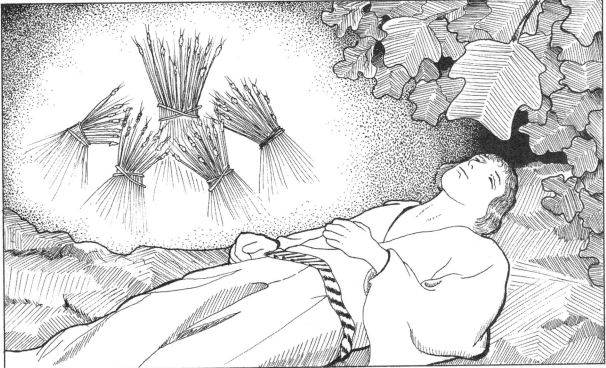

[15]A man found Joseph wandering in the fields. He asked him, "What are you looking for?"

[16]Joseph answered, "I am looking for my brothers. Can you tell me where they are feeding their sheep?"

[17]The man said, "They went away from here. I heard them say, 'Let's go to Dothan.' " So Joseph went after his brothers. He found them in Dothan.

In Your Words

1. Why did Israel love Joseph more than any of his other sons?

2. How did Joseph's brothers act when he told them about his dream? How did his father act?

3. How do you feel when someone else is chosen to do something special? What do you do when you are not that special choice? Are Joseph's brothers happy about his dreams? What do you think they will do to him?

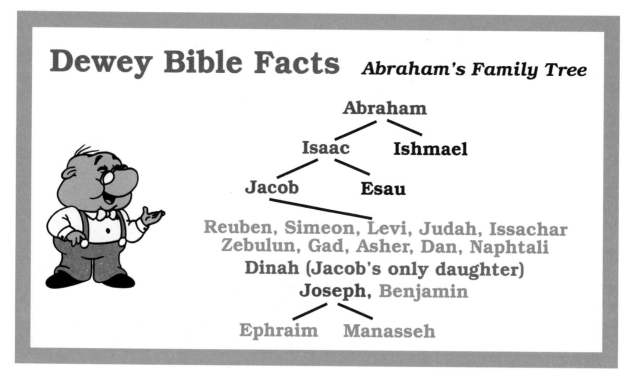

Dewey Bible Facts   *Abraham's Family Tree*

Abraham

Isaac   Ishmael

Jacob   Esau

Reuben, Simeon, Levi, Judah, Issachar
Zebulun, Gad, Asher, Dan, Naphtali
Dinah (Jacob's only daughter)
Joseph, Benjamin

Ephraim   Manasseh

14
Joseph Sold as a Slave

Remember Cain and Abel? Those two brothers didn't get along very well. But Abel had just one brother who hated him. Joseph had eleven brothers who hated him! At their house it was everybody against Joseph. It must have been hard for Joseph. He chose to do what was right. His brothers chose to do what was wrong. One day they chose to do something very wrong. They thought they could keep it a secret. They were wrong.

In Other Words

caravan. Today, our packages travel from place to place. But we don't go with them. In Bible times, traders had to travel from place to place with their packages. Some people spent their whole lives going from place to place buying things and selling things. That's how they made their living. It was exciting when the caravan came to your town.

cistern. In Bible times people did not have water pipes. Sometimes they kept their water in a cistern. It is a large pit for catching rain water.

Jacob/Israel. Names are important to God. God changed Jacob's name to Israel. The name "Israel" means "he struggles with God."

Sackcloth is rough, scratchy cloth that people would wear when they were very sad. When they were crying for someone in their family who died they would wear sackcloth.

In God's Words
Genesis 37:18-36

¹⁸While he was still far away, Joseph's brothers saw him. Before he came to them, they planned to kill him.

¹⁹His brothers said, "Here comes that dreamer! ²⁰Let's kill him! Then let's throw him into a **cistern**. We can say that a wild animal ate him up. Then we will see if his dreams come true!"

²¹Reuben (the oldest brother) heard this. He wanted to save Joseph. He said, "Let's not kill Joseph. ²²Do not even hurt him and make him bleed. Throw him into this cistern here in the desert. But do not hurt him." Reuben said this to save Joseph from his brothers. He wanted to take him back to his father.

²³When Joseph came to his brothers, they tore off his robe. (This was the special robe he was wearing.) ²⁴They took him and threw him into the cistern. The cistern was empty. There was no water in it.

²⁵Later, they sat down to eat their food. They saw a **caravan** of Ishmaelites coming from Gilead. Their camels carried many valuable things. They carried spices, balm, and myrrh. They were on their way down to Egypt.

²⁶Judah said to his brothers, "What will we get if we kill our brother and cover up his blood? ²⁷Let's sell him to the Ishmaelites. Let's not hurt him, because he is our brother. He is our own flesh and blood." So his brothers listened to him.

²⁸The Midianites came by. They were men who bought things in one place and sold them in another place. Joseph's brothers pulled him up out of the cistern. They sold him to the Ishmaelites for twenty pieces of silver. The Ishmaelites took Joseph to Egypt.

²⁹Later, Reuben went back to the cistern. He saw that Joseph was not there. He was so sad he tore his clothes. ³⁰He went back to his brothers. He said, "The boy is not there! Where can I go now?"

³¹Then they took Joseph's robe. They killed a goat and dipped the robe in the blood. ³²They took his special robe back to their father. They said, "We found this. Look at it! Is it your son's robe?"

³³**Jacob** (their father, **Israel**) saw that it was Joseph's robe. He cried, "It is my son's robe! A wild animal has eaten him up! It tore Joseph to pieces!"

³⁴Then Jacob tore his clothes and put on **sackcloth**. He cried and was sad about his son for a long time. ³⁵All his sons and daughters came to make him feel better. But he did not want to feel better. He said, "I will be sad until I die. Then I will go down and meet my son in the grave." So his father cried for Joseph.

³⁶The Midianites came to Egypt. They sold Joseph to Potiphar. Potiphar was the captain of the guard. He was a servant of Pharaoh, the king of Egypt.

In Your Words

1. Joseph was sold as a slave. Who bought him and where did they take him?

2. Joseph's brothers thought they could keep what they did a secret. But can we keep a secret from God?

3. How are Joseph's brothers like Cain? How is Joseph like Abel?

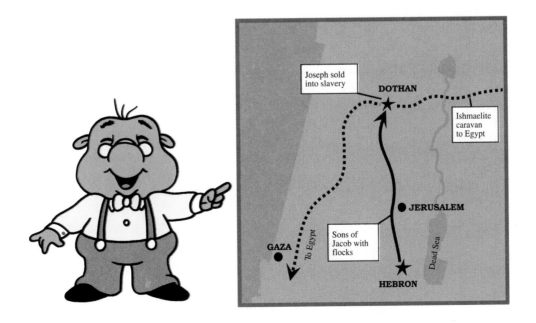

15
Joseph in Egypt

Genesis 39-50

Joseph's brothers were bad! They sold Joseph as a slave. They lied to their father, Jacob. They told him Joseph was dead. Poor old Jacob! Poor young Joseph! Things got worse in Egypt.

Yahweh was with Joseph and helped him. Joseph was Potiphar's best servant. Yahweh blessed Potiphar because of  Joseph. But Potiphar's wife lied to him. She told him that Joseph tried to hurt her. So Potiphar sent Joseph to jail.

Yahweh was with Joseph in jail. Joseph was the best prisoner. He helped the man in charge of the jail.

One day Joseph met two important prisoners. One man was a cupbearer. He brought Pharaoh his food and drink. The other man was Pharaoh's

cook. They told Joseph about their dreams, which they could not understand. But Joseph told them what their dreams meant. He told the cupbearer that he would get his job back. He told the cook he would die. And that is just what happened to both of them!

Two years later, Pharaoh had two very scary dreams. No one could tell him what they meant. His cupbearer remembered Joseph. Pharaoh got Joseph out of jail. God told Joseph what the dreams meant. Joseph told Pharaoh. Pharaoh was so happy he put Joseph in charge of all of Egypt!

Pharaoh's dreams told Joseph what was going to happen. For seven years, farmers grew lots of food. Joseph took much of this food and saved it. After these seven years came seven years when no food would grow. Then Joseph sold the people the food he had saved.

There was no food where Joseph's father and brothers lived. Jacob sent his sons to Egypt to buy food. They bought food from Joseph, but they did not know it was him! Some time later, Joseph's brothers came to buy food again. This time he told them who he was! They brought Jacob and all their families down to Egypt to live with Joseph. How happy Jacob was to live with his son Joseph until he died!

16
God Turns Bad to Good

Have you ever had a dream come true? Joseph did. Remember the dream where Joseph's bunch of grain stood up? And his brothers' bunches of grain bowed down. Guess what? Joseph's brothers are now bowing down to him. His eleven brothers who threw him into the empty cistern are now wanting to be his slaves! Sometimes God takes bad things and makes them good. Things are very good for Joseph. God is blessing him.

In Other Words

forgive. Someone does something to hurt you. You can get even. You can pay him back. You can try to hurt him. Or you can forgive him. That means you won't get even, or pay him back, or hurt him.

In God's Words
Genesis 50:15-21

[15]Joseph's brothers saw that their father, Jacob, was dead. They said, "What if Joseph is still mad at us? What if he pays us back for all the bad things we did to him?" [16]They sent Joseph a message. They said, "This is what your father said before he died. He said, [17]'Tell this to Joseph. Please forgive your brothers! Forgive the sins and the evil things they did. They were very bad to you.' So now, please forgive our sins! We are the servants of your father's God." Joseph heard their message, and he cried.

[18]His brothers came to him. They bowed down before him. They said, "We are your slaves."

[19]But Joseph said to them, "Do not be afraid. Should I act like God? [20]You wanted to do bad things to me. But God wanted to do good things. That is what he is doing now. He is saving many lives. [21]So do not be afraid. I will take good care of you and your children." Joseph made them feel better. He said nice things to them.

In Your Words

1. Why were Joseph's brothers afraid of him now that their father was dead?

2. How did Joseph treat his brothers after they threw him into the empty cistern in the desert?

3. Is it better to forgive or to get even? Why?

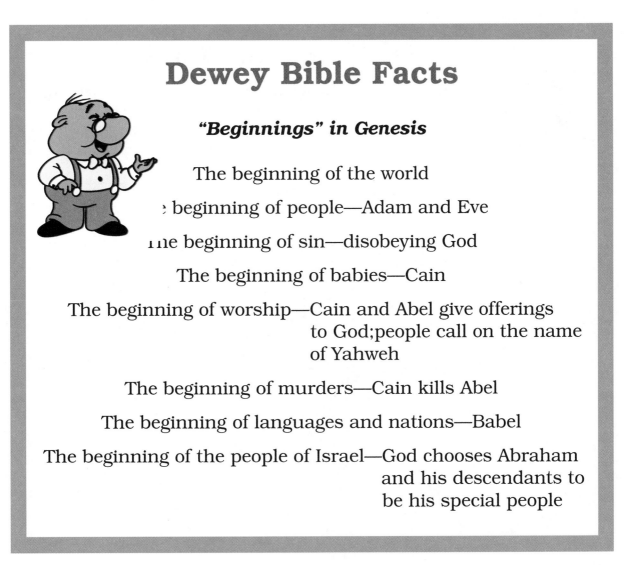

Dewey Bible Facts

"Beginnings" in Genesis

The beginning of the world

beginning of people—Adam and Eve

The beginning of sin—disobeying God

The beginning of babies—Cain

The beginning of worship—Cain and Abel give offerings to God; people call on the name of Yahweh

The beginning of murders—Cain kills Abel

The beginning of languages and nations—Babel

The beginning of the people of Israel—God chooses Abraham and his descendants to be his special people

17
Egypt Makes Slaves of the Israelites

God told Adam and Eve to have many children and fill the earth. He told Noah to have many children and fill the earth. Now look at this. The **Israelites** are having many children. They are filling the earth. More and more babies are being born every day. God is blessing the Israelites.

Pharaoh doesn't like it. He works the Israelites harder. He tells the **midwives** to kill all the boy babies. He tells the people to throw their boy babies into the river! But Pharaoh isn't as strong as God. And God is blessing the Israelites.

In Other Words

Hebrew. A Hebrew is another word for Israelite.

Israelite. Children of Israel are Israelites. They

are the descendants of Jacob. Joseph and his brothers were Israelites. All of their children were Israelites.

midwife. A woman whose job is to help mothers give birth to their babies.

Pharaoh. The special name for the king of Egypt.

Slavery is not like having a job. It's life or death. If you work for your master you live. If you don't work for your master you die.

In God's Words
Exodus 1:6-22

⁶Joseph and his brothers and all the people of their age died. ⁷But their children, the Israelites, had many, many children. They grew larger and larger. There were so many of them, the land was filled with them.

⁸Then a man became the new king of Egypt. This man did not know about Joseph. ⁹He said to his people, "Look at all the Israelites! There are more of them than there are of us! ¹⁰We must be very careful with them or they will grow even larger. If there is a war, they will join our enemies. They will fight against us. They will leave our country."

¹¹So the Egyptians put masters over the Israelites. The masters were mean and made them work as **slaves**. The Israelites built cities for **Pharaoh** to keep things in. The cities were Pithom and Rameses.

¹²The Egyptians were mean to the Israelites. But the people kept growing and filling the land! So the Egyptians were afraid of the Israelites. ¹³They made them work even harder. ¹⁴The Egyptians

57

made them very sad. They made the Israelites work very hard. They worked with bricks and mortar. They worked in the fields. The Egyptians were mean to the Israelites everywhere they worked.

[15]The king of Egypt talked to the **Hebrew** midwives. Their names were Shiphrah and Puah. [16]He said, "You help the Hebrew women have babies. Watch carefully when the baby is born. If it is a boy, kill him! But if it is a girl, you can let her live."

[17]The midwives feared God. They did not do what the king of Egypt told them. They let the boys live, too. [18]The king of Egypt called for the midwives. He asked them, "Why did you do this? Why did you let the boys live?"

[19]The midwives answered Pharaoh. They said, "Hebrew women are not like Egyptian women. Hebrew women are very strong. They have their babies before we get there!"

[20]So God was good to the midwives. And the people kept growing and growing! [21]The midwives feared God. So God gave them families of their own.

[22]Then Pharaoh gave this order to all his people: "Every Hebrew boy that is born you must throw into the Nile River. But let every girl live."

In Your Words

1. Why doesn't Pharaoh want the Israelites to have more boy babies?

2. What were the names of the two Hebrew midwives? What happened to them when they didn't kill the boy babies like Pharaoh told them to do?

3. How can you tell that the midwives feared God?

18
Meet Moses

God kept Noah and his family alive in a big wooden boat. Now God is keeping Moses alive in a tiny basket boat. Pharaoh told the Israelites to throw their boy babies into the river. Well, Moses' mother threw him into the river. She just put him in a tiny basket boat first. So he didn't drown in the river. God kept him alive. God had special plans for Moses.

In Other Words

concern. When someone is concerned, he cares. Sometimes the people of Israel feel like God doesn't care when they hurt. But God does care. He always knows what is happening to them. He is always ready to help them.

Levi/Levite. Levi was one of the twelve sons of Jacob. Moses and his brother were Levites. They would one day help God's people worship God in the right way.

papyrus. A plant that grows in the water. It was used to make baskets and sheets of paper.

In God's Words
Exodus 2:1-15a

¹There was a man from the family of **Levi**. He married a woman from the family of Levi. ²The woman became pregnant and had a son. She saw that he was a fine baby. So she hid him for three months. ³Soon she could hide him no more. She got a **papyrus** basket for him. She covered it with tar and pitch. She put her baby in the basket. Then she put the basket in the Nile River, in the grass that grew at the side of the river. ⁴The baby's sister stood near

by. She wanted to see what would happen to the baby.

[5]Then Pharaoh's daughter came down to the Nile River. She came to take a bath. Her servant girls were walking along the side of the river. Pharaoh's daughter saw the basket in the river grass. So she sent her servant girl to get it. [6]Pharaoh's daughter opened the basket. She saw the baby. He was crying, and she felt sorry for him. She said, "This is one of the Hebrew babies."

[7]Then the baby's sister talked to Pharaoh's daughter. She said, "Would you like me to go and get a Hebrew woman for you? I could get a woman to nurse the baby for you."

[8]Pharaoh's daughter said, "Yes, go!" So the girl went and got the baby's own mother. [9]Pharaoh's daughter said to the woman, "Take this baby and nurse him for me. I will pay you for doing this." So the woman took her baby and nursed him.

[10]The child grew older. So the woman took him to Pharaoh's daughter, and he became her son. Pharaoh's daughter named him Moses. She said, "I took him out of the water."

[11]Years later, Moses was a grown-up. He went out to see his people, the Hebrews. He saw them working very hard. He saw an Egyptian hitting a Hebrew man. The Hebrew was one of Moses' people. [12]Moses looked around. He saw that no one was watching. He killed the Egyptian and hid him in the sand.

[13]The next day Moses went out again. He saw two Hebrews fighting. One of the men was doing wrong. Moses asked him, "Why are you hitting one of your own people?"

[14]The man said, "Who made you our ruler? Who made you our judge? Are you planning to kill me like you killed the Egyptian?" Then Moses was scared. He thought, "Oh no! Everyone knows what I did!"

[15]Pharaoh heard of what Moses did. He tried to kill Moses. But Moses ran away from Pharaoh. He went to live in the land of Midian.

Exodus 2:23-25

²³Many years later, the king of Egypt died. The Israelites groaned because they were slaves. They cried out because they were slaves. Their cry for help went up to God. ²⁴God heard them crying. God remembered his covenant with Abraham, with Isaac, and with Jacob. ²⁵So God looked on the Israelites. And God was **concerned** about them.

In Your Words

1. Who adopted Moses as her own son?

2. Why did Moses go to Midian?

3. Sometimes the leaders of a country do not do what is good. If they ask you to disobey God, what should you do?

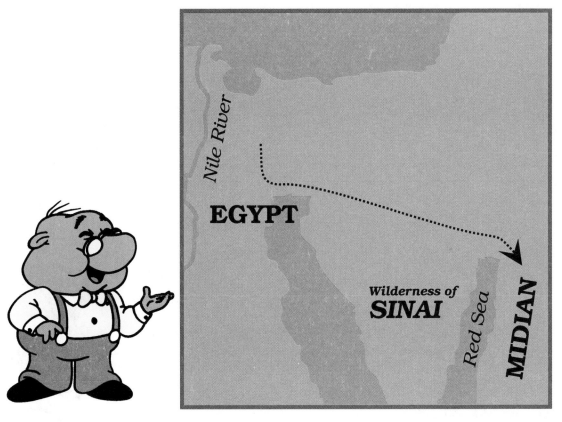

19
God Explains His Name

Names are interesting. Lot's name is short. Zerubbabel's name is very, very long. When God names someone, the name tells us something about the person. In the Hebrew language Adam sounds like the word for ground. Remember how God made Adam from the ground? Abraham means "father of many." Isaac means "he laughs."

So when God tells us the name he wants to be remembered by, we need to listen carefully. His name is **Yahweh**. His name means that he is always with us and he saves us. And that is exactly what he does for us.

In Other Words

priest. A man who leads people in their worship of God. He prays for them. He blesses them. And he makes offerings for them.

Yahweh is God's special name. God explains that "Yahweh" means "I am who I am." His name tells us that he is always with us and that he saves us. He wants to be remembered by this name always.

 ## In God's Words
Exodus 3:1-15

¹Moses took care of Jethro's sheep. Jethro was the **priest** of Midian. Moses had married one of Jethro's daughters. Moses led the sheep across the desert. He came to Horeb, the mountain of God. ²The angel of **Yahweh** appeared to Moses. The angel was in the flames of a burning bush. Moses saw that the bush was on fire, but it did not burn up. ³So Moses thought, "I will go and see this strange thing. I wonder why this bush does not burn up?"

⁴Yahweh saw that Moses had gone to look at the bush. So God called to him from the bush, "Moses! Moses!"

Moses said, "Here I am."

⁵God said, "Do not come any closer. Take off your sandals. You are standing on holy ground." ⁶Then God said, "I am the God of your father. I am the God of Abraham, the God of Isaac, and the God of Jacob." Then Moses covered his face. He was afraid to look at God.

⁷Yahweh said, "I have seen my people in Egypt. I have seen their troubles. I have heard them crying out because of their slave masters. I am concerned about their pain. ⁸So I have come down to rescue them from the Egyptians! I will bring them out of that land. I will take them into a good land. This land has lots of room. This land is filled with good food—like milk and honey. This land is now the home of the Canaanites, Hittites, Amorites, Perizzites, Hivites, and Jebusites. ⁹Yes! The cry of the Israelites has come to me. I have seen that the Egyptians are very mean to them. ¹⁰Now I want you to go. I am sending you to Pharaoh. Bring my people the Israelites out of Egypt!"

¹¹But Moses said to God, "Who am I? Why should I go to Pharaoh? How can I bring the Israelites out of Egypt?"

¹²God said, "I will be with you. And this will prove to you that I

have sent you: You will succeed. You will bring the people out of Egypt. You will worship God on this mountain."

[13]Moses said to God, "I will go to the Israelites. I will tell them, 'The God of your fathers has sent me to you.' But they will ask me, 'What is his name?' Then what should I tell them?"

[14]God said to Moses, "I AM WHO I AM. Say this to the Israelites: 'I AM has sent me to you.'" [15]God also said to Moses, "Say this to the Israelites: 'Yahweh is the God of your fathers. He is the God of Abraham, the God of Isaac, and the God of Jacob. Yahweh has sent me to you.' Yahweh is my name forever. All people for all time will know me by my name Yahweh."

In Your Words

1. Imagine a bush on fire that never burns to ashes! I've never seen such a thing. Have you? Why do you think the bush did not burn up?

2. Why would Moses be afraid to go back to Egypt and tell Pharaoh to let the Israelites go?

3. What is God's name? What does his name mean? How long does he want us to remember him by that name?

20
Moses Goes Back to Egypt

How would you like to have a walking stick? A very different kind of walking stick? Just think, a walking stick that turned into a snake—when you wanted it to. People would think that you had  special powers. They would wonder where you got the stick. If you told them you got the stick from God, they would believe that God was very strong.

Moses had a stick like that. God gave it to him as a **sign**. And with a stick like that, the people believed that God sent Moses to them. They were happy that God remembered them. They were glad that he wanted to help them. They listened carefully to Moses.

In Other Words

Signs are "miracles." Sometimes God does signs for people. He wants to show us that he is the one sending a message. He wants us to be sure that a person who says he is from God is really from God. Signs are unusual. They don't work the way things usually work. A stick that becomes a snake is not usual. It is a sign.

In God's Words
Exodus 3:16-22

[16]God said to Moses, "Go! Bring together the leaders of Israel. Say to them, 'Yahweh, the God of your fathers, appeared to me. He is the God of Abraham, Isaac, and Jacob. He said: I have been watching over you. I have seen what has happened to you in Egypt. [17]I promise I will bring you out of your troubles in Egypt. I will take you into the land of the Canaanites, Hittites, Amorites, Perizzites, Hivites, and Jebusites. This land is filled with good food—like milk and honey.'

[18]"The leaders of Israel will listen to you. Then you and the leaders must go to the king of Egypt. Say to him, 'Yahweh, the God of the Hebrews, has met with us. Please let us go into the desert for

three days. There we will offer sacrifices to Yahweh our God.' ¹⁹But I know that the king of Egypt will not let you go. A strong hand must force him to let you go. ²⁰So I will reach down with my hand. I will strike the Egyptians. I will do many wonderful things among them. After that, the king will let you go.

²¹"I will change the Egyptians' feelings. Then they will like the people of Israel. I will do this so that you will not leave as poor people. ²²Every Hebrew woman must talk to her Egyptian neighbor. She must also talk to any Egyptian woman living in her house. She must ask them for things made of silver and gold. She must ask for clothing. Put these things on your sons and daughters. This is how you will take things from the Egyptians."

Exodus 4:27-31

²⁷Back in Egypt, Yahweh spoke to Aaron, Moses' brother. He said, "Go into the desert to meet Moses." Aaron met Moses at the mountain of God and kissed him. ²⁸Moses told Aaron everything Yahweh sent him to say. Moses also told him about all the signs Yahweh commanded him to do. ²⁹Moses and Aaron brought together all the leaders of the Israelites. ³⁰Aaron told them everything Yahweh had told Moses. Moses did all the signs for the people. ³¹So the people believed. They heard that Yahweh was watching over them and had seen their troubles. So they bowed down and worshiped him.

In Your Words

1. How did the Israelites take things from the Egyptians?

2. Moses and Aaron met the people of Israel. _____ did all the talking. _____ did all the signs.

3. Why did the people of Israel bow down and worship Yahweh? What are some of the reasons why you worship Yahweh?

21
Yahweh Punishes Egypt

Pharaoh lived in a beautiful palace. It was beautiful, until . . .

There were flies in the palace. They covered the walls. There were frogs in his bedroom. There were frogs in his hall. Gnats in his eyebrows. And gnats in his ears. And if that wasn't enough, "Is that thunder I hear?" The hail smashed all the plants. It made all the trees bare. And then millions and millions of grasshoppers appeared. Pharaoh's beautiful palace wasn't beautiful now. All was destroyed. Pharaoh told Moses to go!

In Other Words

firstborn. The child born first in any family is special. Israel is God's firstborn. They are the first people God chose to be his special nation. Because the Egyptians tried to kill God's firstborn, God punished them by killing their firstborn sons.

locust. A locust is a large grasshopper.

In God's Words

Psalm 105:23-38

23Israel went to Egypt.
   Jacob lived as a stranger in the land of Ham.
24Yahweh made his people have many children.
   He made them much larger than their enemies.
25Yahweh changed the Egyptians' feelings, so they hated his
      people.
   They made evil plans against his servants.
26Yahweh sent Moses his servant.
   He also sent Aaron, the man he chose.
27They did signs from God in Egypt.
   They did wonderful things in the land of Egypt.
28Yahweh sent darkness and made the land dark.
   He did this because the Egyptians did not do what he had
      asked.
29Yahweh turned their water into blood.
   This made the fish die.
30Their land was filled with frogs.
   They even went into the bedroom of the king!
31Yahweh spoke, and the flies came.
   Bugs were all over the land of Egypt.

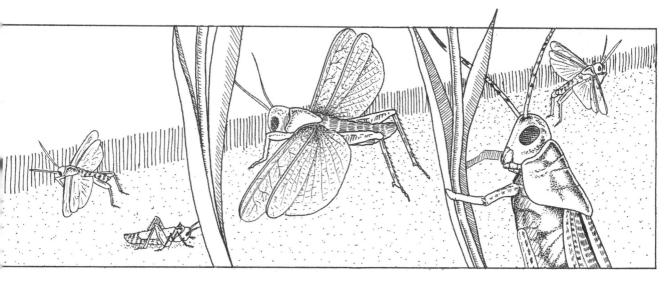

[32]Yahweh turned their rain into hail.
Lightning was all over their land.
[33]Yahweh knocked down their grape vines and fig trees.
He broke down the trees in the land of Egypt.
[34]Yahweh spoke, and the **locusts** came.
There were too many grasshoppers to count!

[35]The locusts ate up every green plant in the land.
They ate up everything that grew from the ground.
[36]Yahweh killed the **firstborn** of each family in Egypt.
The firstborn were their pride and joy.
[37]Yahweh brought out Israel. They took silver and gold with them.
No one from any family tripped or fell down.
[38]Egypt was glad when they left.
They were very much afraid of Israel.

In Your Words

1. Where did Jacob live as a stranger?

2. What were three of the wonderful things God sent Moses and Aaron to do in Egypt?

3. Draw a picture of Pharaoh's palace when it was attacked by the signs from God.

22
Yahweh Is a Warrior

You probably have a hallway in your house. Maybe it joins your living room with your bedroom. If you stretch out your arms in your hallway, you touch hard walls. Imagine stretching out your arms and touching walls made of water. Your hands would get wet. But your body would stay dry. You could walk from your living room to your bedroom without getting wet. Maybe a fish would swim up to you. It would swim to the edge of the wall. But it wouldn't fall into the hallway. You'd feel like you were standing on the ocean floor!

Moses and the Israelites walked through a hallway like that. It was a big hallway in the Red Sea. The Egyptians on their horses and chariots tried to follow them through the hallway in the Red Sea. They wanted to hurt the Israelites. But God made the hallway crash in on them. The walls of water fell down on them. They all died. God was with the Israelites. He saved them from the Egyptians.

In Other Words

holy place. Remember that holy means "different." But it is different God's way. A holy place is a different place used to worship God.

warrior. Someone who fights in wars. A soldier

In God's Words
Exodus 15:1-13

[1]Moses and the Israelites sang this song to Yahweh:

"I will sing to Yahweh,
    for he is high above me.
The horse and its rider
    Yahweh threw into the sea.
[2]Yahweh makes me strong and he makes me sing.
    Yahweh saves me.

Yahweh is a Warrior

He is my God, and I will praise him.
   He is my father's God, and I will honor him.
³Yahweh is a **warrior**.
   Yahweh is his name.
⁴Pharaoh's chariots and his army
   Yahweh threw into the sea.
Pharaoh's best soldiers
   are drowned in the Red Sea.

⁵The deep waters covered the Egyptians.
   They sank to the bottom like a stone.
⁶"Yahweh, your right hand
   is wonderful and strong.
Yahweh, your right hand
   smashed the enemy.
⁷Because you are great and wonderful
   you threw down your enemies.
You sent your burning anger;
   it burned up your enemies like dry grass.
⁸You blew out a great wind!
   You piled up the water.
The waves stood still like a wall.
   The deep water froze like ice in the middle of the sea.
⁹"The enemy said,
   'I will chase them. I will catch them.
I will take away all their things.
   I will take all I want!
I will grab my sword.

   I will kill them with my own hand.'
¹⁰But you blew a great wind!
   You blew the sea over them.
They sank like lead
   in the mighty water.

¹¹"Are there any gods like you, Yahweh?
   Who is like you?
   Only you are wonderful and holy!

Only you are awesome and amazing!
Only you do signs!
[12]You reached out your right hand.
You made the earth swallow your enemies.
[13]"In your great love you will lead
the people you have saved.
In your strength you will take them
to the **holy place** where you live.

In Your Words

1. Who did God drown in the Red Sea?

2. Name five things from this song that describe what Yahweh is like.

3. Why are Moses and the Israelites singing to God? If you were going to write a song about what God does for you, what kind of things would you sing about?

23
God's Covenant with the Israelites

Do you have a favorite shirt? Maybe you have a favorite toy. You might even have a favorite book. Out of all of your things, one thing is the best. It is your special treasure.

The people of Israel are God's special treasure. He made a covenant with them. It was different from his covenant with Noah. It was different from his covenant with Abraham. This time, if the people didn't keep the covenant then God wouldn't keep the covenant. God made a covenant with the people of Israel because he loved them. He wanted to show them how to live happy lives.

In God's Words
Exodus 19:1-9

 ¹Three months after the Israelites left Egypt, they came to the Desert of Sinai. ²They left Rephidim and they came to the Desert of Sinai. The Israelites made their camp in the desert. They camped in front of the mountain.

³Moses went up the mountain to meet with God. Yahweh called to him from the mountain. He said, "Say this to the family of Jacob. Tell this to the Israelites: ⁴'You all saw what I did to Egypt. I was like an eagle; I carried you on my wings. I brought you here to be with me. ⁵So now, do everything I say! Obey my covenant! If you do, then you will be my special treasure. You will be more special than any other people. The whole earth is mine. ⁶But you will be my kingdom of priests. You will be my holy people.' Say these words to the Israelites."

⁷So Moses went back and called for the leaders of the people. He told them all the words Yahweh had commanded him to say. ⁸The people all answered together, "We will do everything Yahweh has said." Then Moses took their answer back to Yahweh.

⁹Yahweh said to Moses, "I will come to you in a dark cloud. The people will hear me when I talk to you. And then they will always believe what you say." Then Moses told Yahweh what the people had said.

74

Deuteronomy 6:4-9

[4]Hear this, people of Israel: Yahweh is our God! Yahweh is the Only One! [5]Love Yahweh your God with all your heart, with all your soul, and with all your strength.

[6]Today I am giving you these commandments. Learn them and keep them in your hearts. [7]Teach the commandments to your children. Talk about them when you sit at home and when you walk along the road. Talk about them when you lie down and when you get up. [8]Write the commandments down. Tie them on your hands so you will remember to do them. Tie them on your foreheads. [9]Write them on the doors of your house. Write them on the gates of your city.

In Your Words

1. Where did Moses go to meet God?

2. What did Israel have to do to be God's special treasure?

3. God wants us to write his commandments down. He wants us to tie them on our hands so we will remember to do them. He wants us to tie them on our foreheads. That means he wants us to memorize them. Pick a verse out of Exodus 19:1-9. Memorize it. Then remember to tie it to your hand. Remember to do what it says.

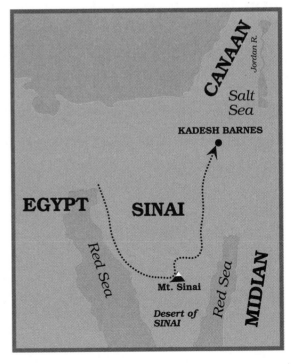

75

24
The Ten Commandments

Look both ways before you cross the street. Don't get into a stranger's car. Eat your spinach! These are all commands. They are commandments. Sometimes they tell us to do something good. Sometimes they tell us not to do something bad. Commandments help us do the right things. Our parents give us commands because they love us. And God gives us commands because he loves us, too.

In Other Words

adultery is having sexual relations with someone else's husband or wife. God says adultery is wrong.

covet. If you want something bad enough to steal it, that is coveting.

Idols are make-believe gods. Some people make things out of wood or metal and say those things are gods. Only Yahweh is God.

murder. If a person kills another person just because he wants to, that is murder. In the Bible, God sometimes commanded his people to kill other people in war. God sometimes commanded his people to kill other people as punishment for their sin. This is not murder.

Sabbath day. This is the seventh day. When God made the world, he rested on the seventh (Sabbath) day. This made it holy.

In God's Words
Exodus 20:1-17

[1]God spoke all these words:

[2]"I am Yahweh your God. I brought you out of Egypt. I brought you out of that land where you were slaves.

[3]"You must have no other gods. I am your only God.

[4]"You must never make an **idol** for yourself. Never make an idol that looks like anything in the sky, or on the earth, or in the water. [5]Never bow down to idols or worship them. I am Yahweh your God. I am a jealous God. If anyone sins against me, I will punish him and his children. I will punish his grandchildren and their children, if they also hate me. [6]But I will show love to thousands and thousands of people if they love me and obey my commandments.

[7]"You must never use the name of Yahweh your God badly. Yahweh will punish anyone who uses his name badly.

[8]"Remember the **Sabbath day**. Make it holy. [9]Do all your work on the other six days of the week. [10]The seventh day is a Sabbath to Yahweh your God. You must never work on the Sabbath. You, your sons and daughters, your men and women slaves must never work on the Sabbath. Even your animals and the strangers who live in your town must never work on the Sabbath. [11]In six days Yahweh made the heavens and the earth, the sea, and all that is in them. But he rested on the seventh day. That is why Yahweh blessed the Sabbath day and made it holy.

[12]"Honor your father and your mother. If you do, you will live for a long time in

the land Yahweh your God is giving you.

¹³"You must never **murder**.

¹⁴"You must never commit **adultery**.

¹⁵"You must never steal.

¹⁶"You must never tell lies about your neighbor.

¹⁷"You must never **covet** your neighbor's house. You must never covet your neighbor's wife, his men or women slaves, his ox or donkey. Never covet anything that your neighbor has."

In Your Words

1. What is the first commandment?

2. Why did God give commandments to his people, the Israelites?

3. If you use God's name to swear at someone, you are using it badly. If you "promise to God" to do something, but you do not do it, you are using his name badly. We should only use God's name when we talk about God and when we sing and pray to him. That is using God's name well.

25
The Golden Calf

Have you ever wondered what God's writing looks like? Moses saw it! He must have been excited when he saw the ten commandments God had written. He had heard God say them. Now he gets to read them.

"You must have no other gods. I am your only God." Moses was glad to read that Yahweh was his only God. But the people wanted other gods. They made an idol from their gold earrings. They melted the gold and formed it in the shape of a calf. The people wanted a gold calf to lead them! Can you believe it?

In Other Words

God changes his mind. God doesn't change his mind like we do. When he changes his mind, it means he changes his actions because people have changed their actions.

Fellowship offerings were like having a special dinner with God—just you and him!

mercy. Help for someone who is in trouble.

In God's Words
Exodus 32:1-16,19-20

¹Moses was on the mountain a long time. (He was talking with God.) The people saw that Moses had not come back down. So they went to Aaron and said, "Make us some gods to lead us. Moses brought us out of Egypt. But we do not know what has happened to him."

²Aaron said to them, "Your wives, your sons and your daughters are wearing gold earrings. Take off their earrings and bring them to

The Golden Calf

me." ³So all the people took off their earrings and brought them to Aaron. ⁴Aaron took their earrings. He melted the gold and used it to make an idol that looked like a calf. He made it with a tool. The people said, "Look, Israel: These are your gods! They brought you out of Egypt."

⁵Aaron saw this. So he built an altar in front of the calf. He told the people, "Tomorrow we will have a special day to worship Yahweh." ⁶So the people got up early the next day. They made burnt offerings and brought **fellowship offerings**. They sat down to eat and drink. But then they got up and did awful, evil things.

⁷So Yahweh told Moses, "Go down the mountain. You brought your people out of Egypt. But your people have turned bad. ⁸They quickly turned away from what I commanded them to do. They made an idol that looks like a calf. They worshiped the idol. They brought it sacrifices. They said, 'Look, Israel: These are your gods! They brought you out of Egypt.' "

⁹Yahweh said to Moses, "I have seen these people. They are stubborn people. ¹⁰So leave me alone! I am angry with these people. I will destroy them. Then I will make you a great nation."

¹¹But Moses asked Yahweh his God for **mercy**. He said, "Yahweh, why should you be angry with your people? You brought them out of Egypt with your great power and your strong hand! ¹²Why should the Egyptians say, 'God had an evil plan against his people. He brought them out of Egypt so he could kill them in the mountains and wipe them off the earth'? Turn away from your great anger! **Change your mind** and do not destroy your people! ¹³Remember your servants Abraham, Isaac, and Israel. You made them a promise by your own life. You said, 'I will give you as many descendants as the stars in the sky. I will give your descendants all the land I promised. The land will belong to them forever.' " ¹⁴So Yahweh changed his mind. He did not destroy his people as he had told Moses.

¹⁵Then Moses went down the mountain. He took the two stone tablets of the Law in his hands. The tablets had writing on both

sides, front and back. [16]God made these tablets. The writing was the writing of God. God himself wrote on the tablets.

[19]Moses came into the camp. He saw the calf and the dancing. Then Moses became very angry. He threw the stone tablets from his hands. He broke them to pieces at the bottom of the mountain. [20]He took the calf the people had made. He burned it in the fire and crushed it into dust. He threw the dust into the water and made the Israelites drink it.

In Your Words

1. Moses broke the stone tablets because the people broke the covenant. Which of the commandments did the people disobey when they made the gold calf? (Look at reading 24.)

2. Who did the people say brought them out of Egypt? Who really brought them out of Egypt?

3. Is Yahweh your only God? Do you love him with all your heart? Why don't you tell him that right now.

26
Yahweh Is a God Who Forgives

God was angry with the Israelites. But he forgave them. Even though they made the gold calf, he still loves them. God would rather bless his children than punish them. But sometimes he has to punish his children. He has to punish his children because he is holy. It's hard to do the right thing all of the time. Isn't it? Aren't you glad that God forgives us when we sin? Aren't you glad God is always with us? There's no other God like Yahweh!

In Other Words

compassionate and **gracious**. God is compassionate when he does good things for people who need help. He is gracious when he does good things for people who don't deserve his help.

full of love and faithfulness. God is always there to do good for those who love and obey him.

repent. We repent when we stop sinning and ask God to forgive us.

slow to anger. God doesn't punish us as soon as we sin. He wants to give us time to **repent**. If we repent, then he doesn't have to punish us.

In God's Words
Exodus 34:1-10

[1]Yahweh said to Moses, "Make two stone tablets like the first ones. I will write on them the words that were on the first tablets, the tablets you broke. [2]Get ready tomorrow morning. Come up on Mount Sinai. Stand before me there on top of the mountain. [3]No one must come with you. No one should be seen anywhere on the mountain. The sheep and cattle may not eat the grass in front of the mountain."

[4]So Moses made two stone tablets like the first ones. He got up early the next morning and went up Mount Sinai. He did all the things Yahweh commanded him. He took the two stone tablets in his hands.

[5]Then Yahweh came down in a cloud and stood there with Moses. He called out his name, Yahweh. [6]Yahweh passed in front of Moses and called out:

83

Yahweh Is a God Who Forgives

"Yahweh, Yahweh, the **compassionate** and gracious God, **slow to anger, full of love and faithfulness,** [7]showing love to thousands, and forgiving wickedness, rebellion, and sin. Yet he does not leave the guilty unpunished. He punishes the children and grandchildren for the sin of the fathers to the third and fourth generation."

[8]Moses quickly bowed to the ground and worshiped God. [9]He said, "Lord, if you are happy with me, then please go with us, Yahweh. These people are stubborn. But please forgive our wickedness and our sin. Take us as your very own."

[10]Then Yahweh said: "I am making a covenant with you. Before all your people I will do wonderful miracles. These miracles have never been done for any other nation in all the world. All your people will see what Yahweh will do. I will do amazing things for you!"

In Your Words

1. God says his name two times in Exodus 34:6 so we will remember what it means. Do you remember what it means?

2. Exodus 34:6,7 is very important to remember. Memorize these verses and remember them often.

27
Israel in the Desert

God wanted his people to go straight from Mount Sinai to the land he had promised to give them. But they would not obey him. Instead they complained and complained. They complained about their leaders. They complained about their food. They even complained about the pleasant land God promised them. So God punished them. He made all the people stay in the desert for forty years. Many, many Israelites came out of Egypt. But only two of those Israelites went into the promised land! All the others died in the desert. Only Joshua and Caleb believed God's promise. They went into the promised land.

In God's Words
Verses from Psalm 106

¹Praise Yahweh!
Give praise to Yahweh, for he is good.
   His love never ends!
¹⁰Yahweh saved our fathers from the hands of their enemies.
   He rescued them from people who hated them.
¹¹The waters covered their enemies.
   None of their enemies got away.
¹²Then our fathers believed Yahweh's promises.
   They sang his praise.

¹³But soon our fathers forgot what Yahweh did.
   They did not listen for his advice.
¹⁴In the desert our fathers wanted special food.
   They tested God to see if he would feed them.
¹⁵God gave them what they asked for.
   But he punished them by making them sick.

[16]In the camp some people were jealous of Moses.

They were jealous of Aaron, Yahweh's chosen servant.

[17]The ground opened up and swallowed Dathan.

It covered the people who followed Abiram.

[18]A fire burned up the people who followed them.

Flames burned up the wicked people.

[24]Then our fathers would not go into the pleasant land.

They did not believe Yahweh's promise.

[25]They complained in their tents.

They did not obey Yahweh.

[26]So Yahweh made them a promise.

He promised that he would let them die in the desert.

[27]He promised that he would let their children die in other lands.

He promised that he would scatter them all over the world.

[28]Our fathers worshiped the make-believe god Baal in Peor.

They ate sacrifices given to gods that are not alive.

[29]They did wicked things that made Yahweh angry.

So he punished them by making them sick.

[32]Our fathers made Yahweh angry by the waters of Meribah.

Moses got in trouble because of them.

[33]They sinned against the Spirit of God.

Even Moses said things that were wrong.

In Your Words

1. Why didn't the people get to go into the pleasant land?

2. What happened to the Israelites in the desert? What good things happen to you when you complain?

3. The people would not obey. Did Moses obey?

28
Love and Obey Yahweh Your God

Sometimes it's hard to remember to clean up your room. Sometimes it's hard to remember to finish your homework. But it really isn't too hard to clean up your room. And it really isn't too hard to finish your homework. God told his people what he wanted them to do. They probably said, "That's too hard for us." But it wasn't too hard for them. He told them how to obey. If they loved him, they would choose to obey him. And if we love God, we will choose to obey him too. We will read his Bible and do what he asks us to do.

In God's Words

Deuteronomy 30:11-20

[11]What I am commanding you today is not too hard for you to do. It is not far away from you. [12]It is not up in heaven. You do not have to ask, "Who will go up to heaven to get God's word? Who will tell us what it means so we may obey it?" [13]It is not across the sea. You do not have to ask, "Who will cross the sea to get God's word? Who will tell us what it means so we may obey it?" [14]No, the word is very near to you. The word is in your mouth and in your heart so you may obey it.

[15]Today I am telling you about life and good things, and about death and bad things. [16]Today I command you to love Yahweh your God and to live the way he wants you to live. Obey his commands, his rules, and his laws. If you love and obey God, you will live and have many children. Yahweh your God will bless you in the land.

(You will soon go into this land and take it as your own.)

¹⁷But your heart might turn away from Yahweh. You might not obey him. You might decide to worship and to obey other gods. ¹⁸Today I tell you that if you do this you will die! You will not live very long in the land. (You will soon cross the Jordan River to go into this land and take it as your own.)

¹⁹Today I ask heaven and earth to remember what you choose. I have told you about life and death, and about blessings and curses. Now choose life so that you and your children may live. ²⁰Choose to love Yahweh your God. Listen to his voice. Stay close to him. For Yahweh is your life. He will let you live many years in the land. (He promised to give this land to your fathers, Abraham, Isaac, and Jacob.)

In Your Words

1. God told the Israelites that his commands were not too hard for them to obey. Read 1 John 5:3 in a Bible. What did John tell the Christians about God's commands?

2. God promised to give Christians a home in heaven. Where did God promise to give the Israelites a home?

3. How do you find out how Yahweh wants you to live? Where can you find out what he wants you to do and what he doesn't want you to do?

29
God's World and His Word

Look up at the sky today. You probably see clouds and birds and sunlight. Look up at the sky tonight. It is filled with stars and planets and the moon. When we look at the sky, it's easy to believe God made all things. It's easy to see his glory. But we can only learn a little bit about God by looking at his sky. We can learn much more about him by reading the Bible. The Bible tells us all about God. It tells us how much he loves us. And it tells us how we can love him, too.

In Other Words

The glory of God is something we can see that tells us what God is like and what he does. Sometimes glory is bright light. Sometimes glory is you and me and the world God made. When we live the way God wants us to live, we show people the glory of God.

Simple people are people who still have a lot to learn. They have not yet decided to be good or bad people. All of you young readers are "simple." You become wise when you choose to follow God's ways as you learn about him.

In God's Words

Psalm 19

For the Song Leader. A psalm of David.

¹The heavens tell of **the glory of God**.
   The sky talks about what his hands have made.
²Day after day their words come down.
   Night after night they say what they know.
³There are no words or sounds.
   No one hears their voice.
⁴Their voice goes all over the world.
   Their words go to the ends of the earth.
In the heavens God set up a tent for the sun.
⁵The sun comes out of its tent like a man who just got married.
   It is as happy as a champion running a race.
⁶The sun comes up at one end of the sky.
   It goes all the way around the other end.
   Nothing can hide from its heat.

⁷The law of Yahweh is perfect.
   It makes people strong inside.
The word of Yahweh is true.
   It makes **simple people** wise.

⁸Yahweh's rules are right.
   They make people happy inside.
Yahweh's commands are clean.
   They light up the way to life.
⁹The fear of Yahweh is pure.
   It goes on forever.
Yahweh's decisions are true.
   They are completely right.
¹⁰The words of Yahweh are worth more than gold.
   They are worth more than pure gold.
They are sweeter than honey.
   They are sweeter than fresh honey.
¹¹They tell your servant what to do.
   You reward your servant for obeying them.

¹²No one knows everything he does wrong.
   Forgive the sins I cannot remember.
¹³Keep your servant from sinning on purpose.
   Do not let sin control me.
Then I will obey perfectly.
   I will be free from the worst sins.
¹⁴I pray that the words of my mouth and the thoughts of my
   heart will please you.
Yahweh, you are my Rock and my Savior.

In Your Words

1. What are simple people like?

2. Your mom and dad probably wear gold wedding rings. Those rings are valuable! What does the psalm say is more valuable than gold?

3. Why do you think David calls Yahweh his rock?

30
Be Strong and Be Brave!

I just invented a new game. Imagine you're standing outside the gate to my playground. It is a fantastic playground. It is the best playground you have ever seen. When I let you through the gate, the game begins. Here's how the game works. Every place you put your foot becomes your playground. If you walk to the swings, they're yours. If you walk to the slide, it's yours too. Every time you walk to a new place, I give you some more of my playground. If you want, you can have the whole playground.

God is going to give the Israelites the pleasant land like I gave you my playground. Every place they put their foot will become their land. The whole land will be theirs!

In Other Words

meditate. When we meditate, we talk to ourselves about what God is like and what he has done. When we tell others what God is like and what he has done, that's praise.

successful. When you do something God wants you to do, you are successful. Joshua was successful because he believed Yahweh. He led Israel to take over the land Yahweh had promised to give them.

In God's Words
Joshua 1:1-9

[1]Moses, the servant of Yahweh, was dead. Joshua, the son of Nun, had been Moses' helper. Yahweh said to Joshua, [2]"Moses my servant is dead. Now get ready. You and all these people go across the Jordan River. Go into the land I am giving to the Israelites. [3]I will give you all the land you walk on. I promised Moses I would do this. [4]All the land from the desert to Lebanon will be yours. All the land of the Hittites, from the big Euphrates River to the big western

sea, will be yours. [5]No one will stand in your way as long as you live. I was with Moses, and I will be with you. I will never leave you. I will never let you down.

[6]"Be strong and be brave! You will lead these people to take over the land. I promised their fathers that I would give the land to these people. [7]Be strong and be very brave! Be sure to obey all of the law that my servant Moses gave you. Do not turn away from my law. Do not turn to the right or to the left. Then you will be **successful**. [8]Do not stop talking about this Book of the Law. **Meditate** on its teaching day and night. Then you will be sure to do everything that is written in the Book. Then everything you do will work out well and you will be successful. [9]Remember what I commanded you. Be strong and be brave! Do not be afraid. Do not be sad. For Yahweh your God will be with you everywhere you go."

In Your Words

1. Moses is dead. Is the gold calf going to lead the people? Who is going to lead God's people?

2. Who will be with Joshua and the Israelites wherever they go?

3. God told Joshua to meditate on his law day and night. Look back to reading 26. You memorized Exodus 34:6,7 in that reading. Now make sure you can say it from memory. Meditate on Exodus 34:6,7. Talk to yourself. Tell yourself what God is like.

31
Israel Sins but Yahweh Saves

Joshua died when he was 110 years old. He led the Israelites well. He reminded them often of God's law. The people listened to God's law and they obeyed it. But now the people don't remember what Yahweh has done. No one is reminding them. Their parents didn't tell them the wonderful things about Yahweh. So they are living like all the other people who don't know Yahweh. They are doing bad things. Oh no! They are worshiping make-believe gods. They are worshiping **Baal** and **Ashtoreth**. Someone needs to remind them that there is no god besides Yahweh.

In Other Words

Baal and **Ashtoreth** were two favorite make-believe gods of the Canaanites. Their ways were evil. The people thought they were mean gods.

generation. A generation is made up of people who are about the same age. The other children in your school are in your generation. Your teachers are in your parents' generation.

In God's Words
Judges 2:7,10-19

⁷The people served Yahweh as long as Joshua lived. Some of their leaders lived longer than Joshua. These leaders had seen all of the great things that Yahweh did for Israel. The people served Yahweh as long as these leaders lived.

¹⁰That whole **generation** died, just like their fathers. Another generation grew up after them. But they did not remember Yahweh. They did not remember the things that Yahweh did for Israel. ¹¹These Israelites did things that Yahweh said were evil. They served the make-believe god Baal. ¹²They turned away from Yahweh. Yahweh was the God of their fathers. Yahweh had brought them

out of Egypt. But these people followed other gods. They worshiped the gods of the people who lived around them. They made Yahweh angry. [13]They turned away from Yahweh. They served the make-believe gods Baal and Ashtoreth.

[14]Yahweh became angry with Israel. He punished them by letting robbers rob them. He let all their enemies beat them. Israel could not stop their enemies from beating them. [15]Every time Israel went out to fight, Yahweh fought against them. Yahweh promised Israel he would do this if they disobeyed him. Things were very bad for Israel.

[16]Then Yahweh gave them great leaders called judges. The judges saved Israel from these robbers. [17]But they would not obey their judges. They followed other gods and worshiped them. These people did not act like their fathers. Their fathers had followed Yahweh and had obeyed his commands. [18]When Israel's enemies did bad things to them, they cried out to Yahweh. Yahweh felt sorry for Israel and gave them a judge. Yahweh was with that judge. He saved Israel from their enemies as long as the judge lived. [19]But when the judge died, the people went back to their old ways. They were worse than their fathers. They followed other gods. They served and worshiped these gods. They did not stop doing evil. They wanted to have their own way.

In Your Words

1. Why did the new generation of Israelites do evil things?

2. Who saved the Israelites from their enemies?

3. What did the people do when a judge who had saved them died?

Dewey Bible Facts

Israel's Judges

ENEMY	JUDGE	TRIBE	YEARS
Mesopotamia	Othniel	Judah	40
Moabites	Ehud	Benjamin	80
Philistines	Shamgar	*Unknown*	10
Canaanites	Deborah	Ephraim	40
Midianites	Gideon	Manasseh	40
	Tola	Issachar	23
	Jair	Gilead	22
Ammonites	Jephthah	Gilead	6
	Ibzan	Judah	8
	Elon	Zebulun	10
	Abdon	Ephraim	7
Philistines	Samson	Dan	20
	Samuel	Ephraim	?

32
Samuel: The Greatest of the Judges

Have you ever met someone who always wanted his own way? He never did what anyone else wanted him to do. Maybe he never did what you wanted him to do. The Israelites wanted their own way. They didn't want to obey Yahweh. So he punished them. Things were very bad for the Israelites. Things were bad until Yahweh gave the people a judge. While a judge was alive, the people were saved from robbers and enemies. The last judge was Samuel. He loved and obeyed Yahweh. He was the greatest judge.

In Other Words

from Dan to Beersheba. The city of Dan is at the "top" of Israel in the north. Beersheba is at the "bottom" in the south. "From Dan to Beersheba" means the whole land and all the people of Israel.

reveal, revelation. God is invisible. We cannot see him. We only know what he is like and what he wants us to do if he reveals himself to us. God has revealed himself in the things he did for Israel. God has revealed himself in the words he spoke to the prophets. God's greatest revelation is in the life and words of his Son, Jesus. We have God's revelation in the Bible.

In God's Words

1 Samuel 3:19-4:1

[19]Yahweh was with Samuel as he grew up. Yahweh made all of Samuel's words come true. [20]All Israel **from Dan to Beersheba** knew that Samuel was a real prophet of Yahweh. [21]Yahweh would meet with Samuel at Shiloh. At Shiloh, Yahweh **revealed** himself to Samuel in the word of Yahweh. [4:1]Samuel's word went to all Israel.

1 Samuel 7:15-17

[15]Samuel was judge over Israel all the days of his life. [16]Every year he went around Israel to be their judge. He went from Bethel to Gilgal to Mizpah. He was the judge over Israel in all those places. [17]He always went back to Ramah. His home was in Ramah. He judged Israel in Ramah, too. He built an altar there to Yahweh.

In Your Words

1. How can we know what God is like? How can we know what he wants us to do?

2. What does the Bible mean when it says "from Dan to Beersheba"?

3. Yahweh was with Samuel as he grew up. Is Yahweh with you as you grow up?

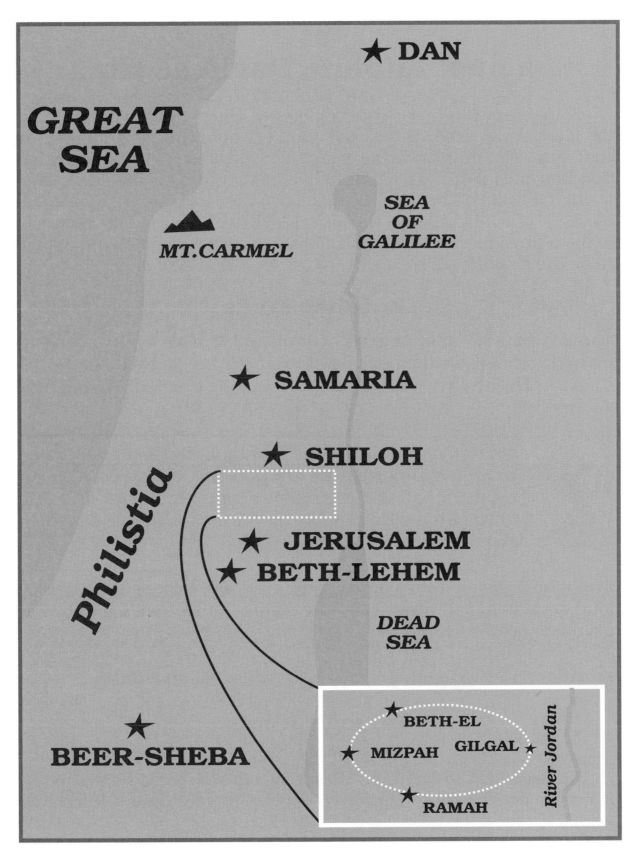

33

Samuel Anoints David as King

Sometimes it's hard to be different. When I was young, I had freckles on my nose. Other kids didn't. I didn't like being different that way. The nations living near the Israelites had human kings. The Israelites didn't. They didn't like being different that way. They wanted a human king, too. So God gave them a king. His name was Saul. He was tall. And he was strong. The people thought he would make a fine king. But he didn't. Then, God chose a young shepherd to be the Israelite's king.

In Other Words

anoint. Samuel anointed both Saul and David. That means he poured olive oil on their heads. The anointing showed the people that the Holy Spirit was coming to make the person strong and successful.

 **heart**. Our heart is where we think and feel and choose. Yahweh knows what we are thinking. He knows if we are happy or sad. He even knows why we choose to do the things we do. He can look at our heart. People can't look at our heart.

ram's horn. Some ram's horns were used like trumpets. They blew loud sounds to call the people to worship. Other ram's horns were used like bottles to hold liquid.

sacrifice. An offering that involves the killing of an animal.

In God's Words
1 Samuel 16:1-13

¹Yahweh said to Samuel, "How long will you be sad about Saul? I have rejected him as king over Israel. Fill your **ram's horn** with

olive oil and go! I am sending you to Jesse who lives in Bethlehem. I have chosen one of his sons to be king."

²But Samuel said, "How can I go? Saul will hear about it and kill me!"

Yahweh said, "Take a calf with you. Say, 'I have come to make a **sacrifice** to Yahweh.' ³Invite Jesse to the sacrifice. I will show you what to do. I will tell you which of his sons you need to **anoint**."

⁴Samuel did what Yahweh said. He went to Bethlehem. The leaders of the town were afraid when they met him. They said, "Do you come in peace?"

⁵Samuel said, "Yes, I come in peace. I have come to make a sacrifice to Yahweh. Make yourselves holy and come to the sacrifice with me." Then he made Jesse and his sons holy and invited them to the sacrifice.

⁶When the men came, Samuel saw Eliab. He thought, "This must be the man Yahweh wants to anoint."

⁷But Yahweh said to Samuel, "Do not think about what he looks

like. Do not think about how tall he is. For I have rejected him. Yahweh does not look at the things people look at. People look at what they can see. But Yahweh looks at a person's **heart**."

8Then Jesse called Abinadab and sent him to Samuel. But Samuel said, "Yahweh has not chosen this one." 9Then Jesse sent Shammah. But Samuel said, "Yahweh has not chosen this one." 10Jesse made seven of his sons walk in front of Samuel. But Samuel said to him, "Yahweh has not chosen these." 11He asked Jesse, "Are these all of your sons?"

Jesse said, "There is still my youngest son. He is taking care of the sheep."

Samuel said, "Send for him. We will not sit down to eat until he gets here."

12So Jesse sent and had his son brought back. He was darkly tanned and very handsome.

Then Yahweh said, "Go and anoint him! He is the one."

13So Samuel took the horn of olive oil. He anointed the boy in front of his brothers. From that day on, the Spirit of Yahweh made David strong.

In Your Words

1. Who told Samuel to anoint David?

2. When God looks at us, he does not look at the things people look at. What does he look at?

3. God looked at Saul's heart. God looked at David's heart. He looks at your heart. Do you have a heart that loves and obeys God? How can you keep your heart right before God?

34
David and Goliath

When David was a strong young man, each nation's army had a champion fighter. Two armies would watch as their champions fought. When one champion won, his whole army won. The Philistines had a champion. His name was Goliath. He was big—almost ten feet tall! No one in Israel's army wanted to fight him. No one wanted to fight him except the young shepherd, David. David was skilled with his sling. And Yahweh was with him. So he killed Goliath. David, the champion of Israel, won the battle. So the whole Israelite army won! Today, Jesus is our champion. When he wins a battle, we win too. And Jesus always wins his battles.

In Other Words

sling. A sling was a long strip of leather with a pocket in the middle. The pocket held a rock. A person swung the sling like a propeller and then let go of one of the ends. The rock then sailed through the air. Golf-ball size rocks traveled up to one hundred yards.

uncircumcised Philistine. The Philistines lived between the Israelites and the sea. They were called uncircumcised because they didn't have a covenant with God like the Israelites did.

In God's Words
1 Samuel 17:34-37; 40-52

³⁴David said to Saul, "I, your servant, take care of my father's sheep. Sometimes a lion or a bear comes and takes a sheep from the flock. ³⁵Then I go after it. I hit it and save the sheep from its mouth. If it turns on me, I grab it by its fur. I hit it and kill it. ³⁶I, your servant, have killed lions and bears. Goliath, this **uncircumcised Philistine**, will be just like them. He will die

because he said evil things about the armies of the living God. [37]Yahweh saved me from the paws of lions and bears. Yahweh will save me from the hands of this Philistine."

Saul said to David, "Go, and may Yahweh be with you."

[40]David took his shepherd's stick in his hand. He chose five smooth stones from the stream and put them in the pocket of his shepherd's bag. He took his sling in his hand and went toward the Philistine.

[41]The Philistine came closer and closer to David. (The man carrying Goliath's shield was in front of him.) [42]Goliath looked at David and hated him. He saw that David was only a boy, tanned and handsome. [43]He said to David, "Am I a dog? Should you come at me with sticks?" The Philistine called to his gods to curse David. [44]Goliath said to David, "Come here! I will feed you to the birds of the sky and to the wild animals!"

[45]David said to the Philistine, "You come against me with your sword, your big spear, and your small spear. But I come against you in the name of Yahweh of the armies of heaven! He is the God

of the armies of Israel. You have said evil things about him. [46]Today Yahweh will give you into my hand. I will knock you down and cut off your head. Today I will feed the bodies of the Philistine army to the birds of the sky and the wild animals. Then the whole world will know that there is a God in Israel. [47]Both of these armies will know that Yahweh does not use swords or spears to save his people. The battle belongs to Yahweh. He will give you and your army into our hands."

[48]The Philistine moved closer to meet David. And David ran quickly to meet Goliath. [49]David reached into his bag and took out a stone. He swung his sling and shot the stone. The stone hit the Philistine and sank into his forehead. Goliath fell on his face to the ground. [50]So David beat the Philistine with a sling and a stone! David knocked Goliath down and killed him with no sword in his hand. [51]David ran and stood over the Philistine. He grabbed Goliath's sword and took it out of his belt. David killed Goliath and cut off his head with the sword. The Philistines saw that their hero was dead. So they ran away. [52]The men of Israel and Judah got up and shouted! They ran after the Philistines all the way to the cities of Gath and Ekron. Many Philistines fell dead all along the way.

In Your Words

1. Goliath's weapons were a sword, a big spear, and a small spear. What were David's weapons?

2. David knew Yahweh was on his side. How did that make him feel?

3. Did David win the battle because he had the best weapons? Why did David win the battle?

35
A Prayer for Help in Time of Trouble

David was brave. Remember how he went after lions and bears? He grabbed them by their fur and hit them and killed them. David was skilled, too. Remember how he used his sling to kill Goliath? He hit Goliath in the head on his first shot. But sometimes David felt alone. Sometimes he felt like nobody cared about him. In the psalms he shows us how he cries out loud to Yahweh for help. And Yahweh answered him. Yahweh made David the new King of Israel. Saul died because he did not obey Yahweh. He did not ask Yahweh for help. Do you ever feel alone? Do you ever feel like people don't like you? Then with all your voice cry to Yahweh. Tell him all about your problems. Tell him about your troubles.

In God's Words
Psalm 142

A psalm about wisdom by David.
When he was in the cave. A prayer.

¹With all my voice I cry to Yahweh.
  With all my voice I ask Yahweh for mercy.
²I tell him all about my problems.
  I tell him about my troubles.
³I'm feeling weaker and weaker.
  But you know where I am.
In the road where I walk
  people hide traps to catch me.
⁴Look at my right side and see!
  No one cares about me.
I have no safe place to stay.
  No one cares if I am alive.
⁵I cry to you, Yahweh!
  I say, "You are my safe place.
  You are all I need in the land of the living."
⁶Listen to my cry,
  for I really need help.

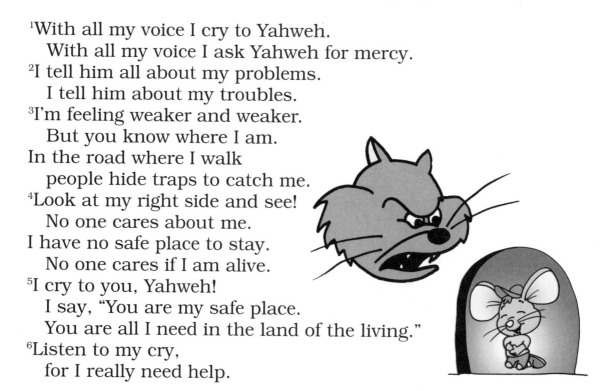

108

Save me from the people who are chasing me,
    for they are too strong for me.
[7]Set me free from this trap,
    so that I may praise your name.
Then people who do what is right will gather around me,
    because you will do good things for me.

In Your Words

1. David is being chased. Where does he say he will find a safe place?

2. When you feel like you need to find a safe place, where can you find it?

3. Do you feel alone? Do you have a problem? You can ask Yahweh for help. Why don't you do so right now.

36
Yahweh Is My Shepherd

Do you ever wake up in the night a little bit scared? It's dark in your room. You wonder if you're home all alone. Then you hear your mom's voice. Maybe you hear your dad's voice too. You're not scared anymore. Once you hear their voices you know that you're not alone. You know that they will take care of you. You go back to sleep.

David had someone to take care of him too. David called this person his shepherd. He was a good shepherd. Sometimes David slept in dangerous places. He probably heard noises in the night. Those noises woke him. But he remembered that his shepherd was with him. That made him feel strong inside. At times like those he was able to go right back to sleep too.

In Other Words

because of his Name. Remember God's name? His name is Yahweh. Remember what Yahweh means? It means God is with us to save us and to help us. Yahweh saves us and helps us because of who he is, because of his Name.

shepherd's rod. This is a large, heavy club shepherds used to fight off lions and bears and wolves. A shepherd used his rod to protect his sheep.

shepherd's staff. This was a stick shepherds used to guide their sheep. A shepherd used his staff to keep his sheep from wandering away and getting lost.

In Bible times, if a special guest came to your house for dinner you would **anoint his head with oil** and wash his feet.

110

111

In God's Words

Psalm 23

A psalm by David.

¹Yahweh is my shepherd.
   I have everything that I need.
²He makes me lie down in soft green grass.
   He leads me by quiet waters.
   ³He makes me strong inside.
He leads me on roads that are good and right
   because of his Name.
⁴Even when I walk
   through the deepest darkest valley
I am not afraid of bad things.
   For you are with me, Yahweh!
Your **shepherd's rod** and your **staff**,
   they make me feel safe.
⁵You make a table full of food for me
   even when my enemies are near.
You **anoint my head with oil**.
   You fill my cup until it runs over.
⁶Yes! Goodness and love will be with me
   as long as I live.
And I will live in Yahweh's house forever!

In Your Words

1. What made David feel safe?

2. How do you think Yahweh the shepherd used his rod and staff to help David?

3. Jesus is our Good Shepherd. He is a strong shepherd. How will you trust him to help you and to save you?

37
God's Promise to King David

Five minutes in a tent is fun. Five days in a tent is okay. But five hundred years in the same old tent? God met the Israelites in the same old tent for almost five hundred years! David wants to build a house for God. He thinks a house will be better than a tent for meeting the Israelites. But God has another idea. God wants to build a house for David. God promises David that one of his descendants will always be the Israelite's king. God's promise makes David happy. So David praises Yahweh, the King of kings!

In Other Words

The ark of God was a wooden box covered with gold. It had two gold angels on its top. It was a model on earth of God's throne in heaven. Sometimes it is called the ark of the covenant.

kingdom. The place where people obey the king is the kingdom. A kingdom lasts only as long as the king and his people are strong enough to defeat those who want to take the kingdom.

name. To have a great name means to be famous. It means to be famous for good things.

In God's Words
2 Samuel 7:1-16

¹King David sat safe in his palace. Yahweh had given him rest from all his enemies around him. ²The king said to Nathan the prophet, "Look at me! I am sitting in a palace made of cedar. But **the ark of God** is sitting in a tent."

³Nathan said to the king, "You are planning something in your heart. Go ahead and do it, for Yahweh is with you."

⁴But that night the word of Yahweh came to Nathan:

⁵"Go and tell my servant David, 'This is what Yahweh says:

God's Promise to King David

Should you build me a house to live in? [6]I have not lived in a house from the day I brought the Israelites out of Egypt to this day. I have lived in a tent as I have gone from place to place. [7]I have gone everywhere the Israelites have gone. I commanded their leaders to take care of my people Israel. But I never said to any of their leaders, "Why haven't you built me a house made of cedar?" '

[8]"So tell my servant David, 'This is what Yahweh of the armies of heaven says: I took you out of the fields. I took you away from the flocks. I made you the leader of my people Israel. [9]I have been with you everywhere you have gone. I have cut down all your enemies. Now I will make your **name** great. Your name will be like the names of the greatest men on earth. [10]I will give my people

Israel their own place. I will plant them so that they stay in their own place. My people will never be bothered again. Wicked people will not hurt them any more, as they did at the beginning. [11]Wicked people have done this ever since I put leaders over my people Israel. I will also give you rest from all your enemies.

"'This is what Yahweh says to you: Yahweh himself will build a house for you! [12]One day your life will be over. You will rest with your fathers. Then I will raise up your son after you. He will come from your own body. I will set up his **kingdom**. [13]He will build a house for my Name. I will set up the throne of his kingdom forever. [14]I will be his father, and he will be my son. When he does wrong, I will punish him the way men punish their children. [15]But I will never take my love away from him, as I took my love away from Saul. (I took Saul away from before you.) [16]Your family and your kingdom will always be in my care. Your throne will stand forever.' "

In Your Words

1. Did Yahweh ever ask the Israelite leaders for a cedar house?

2. How did Yahweh tell David his plan?

3. David's son will be the Israelite's king. How is Yahweh going to treat David's son?

38

A Prayer for God to Forgive Sin

David was a good king. He loved God. And most of the time he obeyed God. But even good people sometimes do bad things. God said, "You must never covet your neighbor's wife." David coveted Bathsheba. She was the wife of his neighbor, Uriah. God said, "You must never commit adultery." David committed adultery. God said, "You must never murder." David murdered Uriah by sending him into a dangerous battle. Do you remember what it means to repent? When you repent, you stop sinning and ask God to forgive you. David did some very bad things. But he repented from his sins. Sometimes you and I do bad things. Just like David, we need to repent. Then God will forgive us just like he forgave David.

In Other Words

Hyssop is a plant that the Israelites used like a brush.

In God's Words
Psalm 51:1-17

For the song leader. A psalm of David.
When the prophet Nathan came to David
after David had committed adultery with Bathsheba.

[1]Have mercy on me, God,
    because of your love that never ends!
Because you care so much,
    wipe away the evil things I have done.

²Wash away all the wicked things I have done.
   Wash me clean from my dirty sin.
³For I know that I have done evil things.
   I always think about my sin.
⁴Against you I have sinned; against you only.
   You saw the evil thing I did.
You are right when you speak against me.
   You are right when you punish me.
⁵Yes, I was sinful when I was born.
   I was sinful even when my mother was pregnant with me.
⁶But you want truth inside me.
   So you teach me to be wise deep inside me.
⁷Brush me clean with **hyssop**, and I will be clean.
   Wash me, and I will be whiter than snow.
⁸Let me hear joy and happiness.
   You punished me; now let my whole body be happy.
⁹Do not look at my sins any more.
   Wipe away all the wicked things I did.
¹⁰Make a pure heart inside me, O God.
   Make my spirit strong, like it was brand new.
¹¹Do not send me away from you.
   Do not take your Holy Spirit from me.
¹²Let me be happy again because you have saved me.
   Make me strong with a spirit that wants to obey you.

¹³Then I will teach evil people to do things your way.
Sinners will turn back to you.
¹⁴Save me from being guilty of murder, God.
You are the God who saves me.
My tongue will sing because you do what is right!
¹⁵Lord, open my lips
and my mouth will shout in praise!
¹⁶If you wanted a sacrifice, I would bring it.
A whole burnt offering does not make you happy.
¹⁷The sacrifices God wants are a broken spirit,
and a broken and humble heart.
These are the sacrifices God accepts.

In Your Words

1. Is Nathan a judge, a king, or a prophet?

2. What does it mean to repent?

3. David said to God, "You are right when you punish me." David wants to learn to always do what pleases God. How does God punish you? Does God's punishment help you learn to do what pleases him? How does it help you learn to do what pleases God?

39
Sing Praise to Yahweh!

When you're on the playground with your friends, **praise** Yahweh. When you're at a restaurant with your mom and dad, praise Yahweh. When you're at school with the other kids, praise Yahweh. When you're at church with all the people, praise Yahweh. Praise Yahweh everywhere with everyone!

In Other Words

Praise is telling others what God is like and what he has done.

In God's Words
Psalm 148

[1]Praise Yahweh!
Praise Yahweh from the heavens.
   Praise him high above the sky.
[2]Praise him, all his angels.
   Praise him, all his armies in heaven.
[3]Praise him, sun and moon.
   Praise him, all you shining stars.
[4]Praise him, high in heaven above.
   Praise him, you waters above the heavens.
[5]Let them all praise the name of Yahweh,
   for he commanded and they were created!
[6]He set them in their places for all time.
[7]Praise Yahweh from the earth.
   Praise him, you giant whales and all the deep sea.
[8]Praise him, lightning and hail, snow and clouds.
   Praise him, you storm winds that do what he wants.
[9]Praise him, you mountains and all hills.
   Praise him, you fruit trees and all cedar trees.
[10]Praise him, you wild animals and all cattle.
   Praise him, you small animals and flying birds.
[11]Praise him, you kings of the earth and all the nations.
   Praise him, you princes and all rulers on earth.

[12]Praise him, young men and women.
  Praise him, old men and children.
[13]Let them praise the name of Yahweh,
  for his name alone is high in honor.
  His beauty is above the earth and the heavens.
[14]He has raised up a king for his people.
  He is the praise of all his holy people.
  He is the praise of Israel, the people close to his heart.
Praise Yahweh!

In Your Words

1. Today, tell at least one person what Yahweh is like.

2. Tomorrow, tell at least one person what Yahweh has done.

40

Yahweh Gives Wisdom to King Solomon

Imagine a world where you got whatever you asked for. Jason asked for a bike. He got a red BMX. Emily asked for a dog. She got a springy, springer spaniel. Benjamin asked for a skateboard. Hey, it was great! Yahweh told Solomon, David's son, "Ask for whatever you want me to give you." Solomon didn't ask for a bike. And he didn't ask for dog. He didn't even ask for a skateboard. Solomon asked for wisdom. And he got wisdom from God. It made him successful.

In Other Words

Wisdom is knowing what is right and doing what is right. When people are wise, they are successful.

In God's Words

1 Kings 3:5-15

⁵Yahweh appeared to Solomon in a dream at night. God said, "I will give you anything you ask for."

⁶Solomon said, "You showed great love to your servant David, my father. He was faithful to you. He did what was right. His heart was right with you. You are still showing this great love to David. You have given him a son to sit on his throne this very day.

⁷"Yahweh my God, you have made your servant king. I have taken the place of my father, David. But I am only a little child. I do not know what to do. ⁸Your servant is here with your people. They are your chosen people. They are a great people. There are too many to count or number. ⁹So give your servant a heart that listens and makes wise choices. Then I can rule your people. Then I can tell what is right and what is wrong. For who can rule this great people of yours?"

[10]The Lord was very happy that Solomon asked for this. [11]So God said to him, "You asked for this. You did not ask for long life. You did not ask to be rich. You did not ask for the death of your enemies. You asked for wisdom to listen and to make wise choices. [12]Because of this, I will do what you have asked. I will give you a wise and understanding heart. You will be wiser than everyone who came before you. You will be wiser than everyone who comes after you. [13]And I will also give you what you did not ask for. I will give you riches and honor. You will be the greatest king of all, as long as you live. [14]And if you walk in my ways, if you obey my rules and my commands as your father David did, I will give you a long life."

[15]Then Solomon woke up. He remembered his dream. He went back to Jerusalem. He stood before the ark of the Lord's covenant and sacrificed burnt offerings and fellowship offerings. Then he gave a feast for all his servants.

In Your Words

1. What did Solomon ask God to give to him?

2. God gave Solomon much more than he asked. What else did God give Solomon?

3. What do you want God to give to you?

41
The Fear of Yahweh

I found hidden treasure.
It wasn't in a sunken ship beneath the raging sea.
And it wasn't in a rusty box below an old oak tree.
I didn't need a treasure map.
And I didn't need a key.
But I found hidden treasure.
Hidden treasure there for me.

What strange hidden treasure am I talking about? The hidden treasure of wisdom. Now it's your turn. Find the hidden treasure in the proverbs of king Solomon.

In Other Words

discipline. When we're taught how to do things God's way, that's discipline. When we're punished for not doing what we're taught, that's discipline, too.

Humility is not thinking you're better than everybody else. When you think you're better than everybody else, that's pride. God likes humility. But he hates pride.

Proverbs are short poems or sayings. They help us know how to live the way God wants us to live.

In God's Words
Selections from **Proverbs**

1:7The fear of Yahweh is the beginning of knowledge.
   Fools hate wisdom and **discipline**.
2:1My son, accept my words.
   Keep my commands with you.
2:2Turn your ear to wisdom.
   Turn your heart to understanding.
2:3Ask for knowledge.
   Call out loud for understanding.
2:4Look for wisdom like you were looking for silver.
   Search for wisdom like you were searching for hidden
      treasure.
2:5And then you will understand the fear of Yahweh.
   Then you will find the knowledge of God.
2:6For Yahweh gives wisdom.
   From his mouth come knowledge and understanding.

3:7Do not think you are wise and already know it all.
   Fear Yahweh and run away from evil.
8:13If you fear Yahweh, you hate evil.
   I hate it when people are proud and stuck-up.
   I hate it when people do bad things and use bad words.
14:16A wise person fears Yahweh and runs away from evil.
   But a fool has a bad temper and is careless.

14:27The fear of Yahweh is a fountain of life.
It saves people from being trapped by death.
19:23The fear of Yahweh leads to life.
There you are safe; trouble does not find you.

15:16It is better to have just a little and to fear Yahweh
than to be very rich and have lots of trouble.
22:4**Humility** and the fear of Yahweh
bring riches and honor and life.

In Your Words

1. What do fools hate?

2. What does it mean to "turn your ear to wisdom"?

3. Do you remember what it means to fear God? (See reading 12.)
What does a wise person who fears Yahweh do? How can you show
that you are wise this week?

42
Wise Parents and Good Children

Who taught you to eat cereal with a spoon? Who taught you to drink milk from a cup? Who taught you to brush your teeth? I think your mom and dad taught you how to do most of these things. Solomon knew that moms and dads teach their children how to do things. And he knew that a boy or girl who listened to his mom and dad would find the hidden treasure. Have you discovered any treasure yet? There's more waiting for you!

In God's Words
Selections from Proverbs

1:8My child, listen to your father's discipline.
　Do not turn away from your mother's teaching.
1:9Their teaching is like a beautiful crown on your head.
　It is like a pretty chain around your neck.
13:1A wise child listens to his father's discipline.
　But a child who talks back does not listen to correction.
23:22Listen to your father; he gave you life.
　Do not hate your mother when she is old.

23:24The man who does right makes his father very glad.
　The parent of a wise child is very happy with him.
10:1A wise child makes his father happy.
　But a foolish child makes his mother sad.
28:7A wise child obeys God's law.
　But a child with selfish friends brings shame to his father.

3:11My child, do not hate Yahweh's discipline.
   Do not get mad when he corrects you.
3:12Because Yahweh disciplines the people he loves.
   This is what a father does to his favorite children.
13:24Parents who do not correct their children hate them.
   But parents who love their children carefully discipline them.
15:5A fool ignores his father's discipline.
   But a wise child listens when he is corrected.
29:15Punishment and correction give wisdom.
   But a child who does what he wants brings shame to his
      mother.

22:6Teach a child the way to live.
   And when he is old he will not turn away from it.
29:17Discipline your child and he will give you peace.
   He will make you happy inside.

In Your Words

1. What is a wise child like?

2. Who does Yahweh discipline? How should you feel about your mom and dad's discipline?

3. How can you make your mom and dad happy inside?

43
Elijah and the Prophets of Baal

Many years after David and Solomon, the people of Israel almost forgot about Yahweh their God. Yahweh had to fight for his people. Yahweh fought the make-believe gods of Egypt when he sent Moses against Pharaoh. Yahweh fought the make-believe gods of the Philistines when he sent David against Goliath. Now Yahweh must fight the make-believe gods of the Canaanites when he sends Elijah against the prophets of Baal.

Ahab was the eighth king of Israel, the northern kingdom. He was the most wicked king Israel ever had. But his wife, Jezebel, was even worse! She wanted Baal to be the God of Israel. She hated Yahweh so much, she tried to kill all the prophets who taught the people to love and obey Yahweh. She sent her own prophets to teach the people to obey the make-believe god Baal.

The most famous prophet of Yahweh at that time was Elijah. He wanted to turn the people back to Yahweh. So he called out to the prophets of Baal. He said, "Let's have a contest to see who is really God!"

One prophet of Yahweh against 450 prophets of Baal seemed like an unfair contest. But the real contest was between the true God, Yahweh, and the make-believe god, Baal! Elijah asked the people of Israel to watch the contest. He said, "If Yahweh is God, follow him! If Baal is God, follow him!"

Elijah made a pile of wood. So did the prophets of Baal. The prophets chose a bull to sacrifice to Baal. Elijah chose a bull to sacrifice to Yahweh. But no one could set fire to the wood. They each had to pray to their God to send fire from the sky. That was the contest! Only a real God could send fire from the sky.

The prophets of Baal shouted and screamed from morning until noon. They danced around their pile of wood and prayed to Baal. But Baal did not answer. Elijah made fun of them. He said, "Shout louder! Maybe your god is busy. Maybe he is on

129

vacation. Maybe he is taking a nap. Shout louder and wake him up!"

The prophets danced and screamed from noon until evening. They cut themselves with knives. (They hoped if they hurt themselves, Baal would answer them.) But Baal did not answer. He made no sound at all. He was not there.

Then Elijah took twelve stones, one for each tribe of Israel. He built an altar to Yahweh. He piled the wood on the altar. He cut up the bull and put it on the wood. Then he had the people pour buckets and buckets of water on top of the altar. Just before dark Elijah prayed to Yahweh. He said, "Yahweh, let the people know that you are God in Israel. Let them know that I am your prophet. Yahweh, answer me! Then the people will know that Yahweh is God. Then the people will turn their hearts back to you!"

Suddenly Yahweh sent fire from the sky! The fire burned up the sacrifice. The fire burned up the wood. The fire burned up the stones and the dirt of the altar. The fire even licked up all the water! All the people fell to the ground. They shouted, "Yahweh! He is God! Yahweh! He is God!"

Yahweh, the real God of Israel, won the contest. The people knew that Baal was no god at all. Then Elijah told the people, "Take all the prophets of Baal! Do not let them get away!"

The people brought the prophets to Elijah. Then, just as the law of Yahweh commanded, Elijah had the prophets killed (see 1 Kings 18:16-40).

Years later, Ahab and Jezebel were killed because they hated Yahweh. But Elijah went up to heaven in a fiery chariot! How much better it is to love and obey Yahweh God!

44
Israel Leaves the Promised Land

The Israelites are turning away from Yahweh's rules again. They are acting like the people around them again. It's hard for the Israelites to be different from the people around them. Isn't it? And it's hard for Christians to be different from the people around them, too. Whenever the Israelites turned away from Yahweh's rules, they acted like the people around them. They acted like the people around them who didn't know Yahweh. And whenever Christians turn away from God's rules in the Bible, they act like the people around them, too. They act like the people around them who don't know Jesus.

In Other Words

Incense was burned like an offering to God or an offering to the make-believe gods. It smelled good.

Israel and Judah. After King Solomon died, the Israelites were split into two kingdoms. The northern kingdom was called Israel. The southern kingdom was called Judah. Neither kingdom loved and obeyed Yahweh. So Yahweh punished them and sent them out of the pleasant land.

Prophets and seers are men and women God spoke to just like he spoke to Moses and Samuel. They often told the people to quit doing bad things, and to love and obey God instead.

In God's Words
2 Kings 17:5-15

[5]The king of Assyria came to the land of Israel. He and his army marched against Samaria. They fought against the city for three years. [6a]In the ninth year of Hoshea (the king of Israel), the king of

Israel Leaves the Promised Land

Assyria won the war with Samaria. He made the Israelites move to Assyria.

[7]All this happened because the Israelites had sinned against Yahweh their God. Yahweh had brought them up out of Egypt. Yahweh had saved them from the power of Pharaoh, king of Egypt. But the Israelites worshiped other gods. [8]They acted like the people that Yahweh moved out of the land before them. The Israelites and their kings did evil things.

[9]The Israelites did secret things against Yahweh their God. These things were not right. They built high places in all their towns so they could worship make-believe gods. They built them in the fields and in the cities. [10]They set up special stones and idols so they could worship Ashtoreth. They put them on every high hill and under every leafy tree. [11]At every high place they burned **incense**. The people that Yahweh moved out of the land before the Israelites did these very things. The Israelites did wicked things. They made Yahweh very angry.

¹²The Israelites worshiped idols. But Yahweh had said, "You must never do this." ¹³Yahweh warned **Israel and Judah**. He had all his **prophets and seers** say, "Turn from your evil ways. Obey my commands and my rules. Do everything that is in the law. I commanded your fathers to obey the law. I gave to you the law from my servants the prophets."

¹⁴But the Israelites would not listen. They were as stubborn as their fathers. Their fathers had not trusted in Yahweh their God. ¹⁵The Israelites turned away from Yahweh's rules. They turned away from the covenant Yahweh had made with their fathers. They turned away from the warnings Yahweh had given them. They followed idols that were good for nothing. So the Israelites became good for nothing, too. They acted like the people around them. But Yahweh had told them, "Do not do what these people do." The Israelites did the things Yahweh had told them not to do.

In Your Words

1. Why did the king of Assyria make the Israelites move to Assyria?

2. What did God's prophets and seers tell the Israelites?

3. How can you make sure not to live like the people around you who don't know Jesus?

45
The Wonderful Child Whose Name Is God

When you were born, your mom and dad probably wrote letters to relatives and friends telling them all about you. They told them your name. They told them your birthday. Your mom and dad even told everbody how much you weighed and how long you were!

One day the people of Israel received a birth announcement. A most amazing birth announcement. It told them all about a new baby. The announcement told them the baby's name. It told them that the baby would be a king. It even told them the name of the baby's family! But it was most unusual. It told the people of Israel all of these things before the baby was even born. This was a most unusual announcement about a most unusual baby.

In Other Words

government. People who are in charge of other people. People who make rules for others to follow.

Wonderful Counselor. A king should be a counselor. He should listen to his people and help them live wisely. But this king is a counselor who is wonderful. He makes us wonder at the things he says and does.

Mighty God. A king should be mighty. He should be strong. This king is not only mighty. He is God!

Eternal Father. A king should be like a father to his people. This king is a father who lives forever.

Prince of Peace. A king should try to give peace to his people. This king will give peace to people he is pleased with.

In God's Words

Isaiah 9:2-3,6-7

²The people who walk in darkness
  see a bright light.
The people who live in the deepest darkness
  see the morning light.
³You have made the nation great.
  You have made them very happy.
The people are happy before you.
    They are as happy as farmers at harvest time.
    They are as glad as soldiers who won the war.
        ⁶For a child is born to us!
            A son is given to us!
        He will be in charge of the **government**.
        And this is his name:
            Wonderful Counselor,
            Mighty God,
            Eternal Father,
            Prince of Peace.
        ⁷His government and peace will grow and grow;
            they will never end.
        He will sit on David's throne.
        He will rule over David's kingdom.
He will build up the kingdom and make it strong.
He will do what is fair and right
  for ever and ever and ever.
Yahweh of the armies of heaven will make this happen
  because he loves his people so very much.

In Your Words

1. What kingdom will this child rule?

2. How can this king's government grow and grow and never end?

3. What kinds of rules will this king make for people to obey? Will you be able to obey them?

46
Daniel and His Friends Trust in God

The people of Israel sinned against Yahweh their God. So Yahweh let the king of Assyria take the Israelites away to Assyria. Yahweh gave the people of Judah more time to turn from their wicked ways. But they sinned against him, too. So Yahweh let the king of Babylon win a war against Judah. The king took the best young men and women away from Judah. He made them live in Babylon. He made them his servants.

The most famous of these men were Daniel and his friends Hananiah, Mishael, and Azariah. These men were wise and strong and handsome. They loved and obeyed Yahweh their God, even though they were slaves in a strange land.

One day, their love for Yahweh got them into trouble! The king of Babylon built a large statue of gold. He made some people play loud music in front of the statue. He told the people of Babylon to bow down and worship the statue when they heard the music. Anyone who did not worship the statue would be burned alive in a red hot furnace!

The king of Babylon moved Daniel and his friends from Judah to Babylon. He changed their names to Belteshazzar, Shadrach, Meshach, and Abednego. But he could not change their love for God. Some people told the king that Shadrach, Meshach, and Abednego would not worship his statue. The king burned with anger—almost as hot as his furnace! He told the three young men that they would be burned alive if they did not obey his command. He asked, "What god is strong enough to save you from my power?"

The three young men said, "The God we obey is able to save us! But even if our God does not save us, we will not obey your gods. We will not worship your golden statue."

The king became very, very angry! He had the furnace made seven times hotter than it was before. He told some soldiers to tie up Shadrach, Meshach, and Abednego and throw them into the

red hot furnace. The fire was so hot that it killed the soldiers when they threw the three young men into the furnace!

But then came the big surprise! The king jumped up and said, "We threw three men into the furnace. But now I see four men in the furnace. They are alive and walking around in the fire! The fourth man looks like a son of God!"

He called to the men, "Shadrach! Meshach! Abednego! You are servants of the Most High God! Praise God who sent his angel to save you! You obeyed God and disobeyed me because you did not want to worship any other gods. Come on out of the fire!"

The king made a law that no one could ever say anything bad about the God of Shadrach, Meshach, and Abednego. Then the king made the three men very important leaders in the land of Babylon (see the Book of Daniel, chapter 3).

47
Daniel Sees the Last Days

Daniel loved and obeyed Yaweh God. But people tried to kill Daniel because he prayed to God. The people threw him into a den of lions! But the lions didn't hurt him. God closed the lions' mouths. Instead of eating Daniel, the lions ate up the wicked people who hated Daniel.

God gave Daniel special dreams and visions. The dreams and visions told him about the future. Daniel saw the last days. He saw times when God's people would be in danger because they loved God. Many people would have to die because they loved God. But Daniel also got to see heaven! He saw that all the people who love and obey God will live with God forever! So even if we die because we love God, God will bring us back to life to live with him forever and ever!

In Other Words

vision. A message God tells a prophet when the prophet is awake.

bronze. A shiny metal. Bronze is a yellow-brown color.

People who love and obey God have their names **written in God's book** of life.

In God's Words

Selections from Daniel 10-12

¹⁰:¹In the third year of Cyrus, the king of Persia, Daniel got a message from God. (Daniel's other name was Belteshazzar.) The message was true. It was about a great war. Daniel saw a **vision** that explained the message. Then Daniel knew what the message meant.

⁵I, Daniel, looked up and saw a man! He wore white linen clothes with a gold belt. ⁶His body shined like a jewel. His face was bright as lightning. His eyes flashed like fire. His arms and legs were like shining **bronze**. His voice sounded like a whole crowd of people.

⁷I, Daniel, was the only one who saw this vision. Some men were with me, but they did not see the man. But they were so scared that they ran away and hid! ⁸I was left alone. I stared at this great vision. I became weak. My face turned pale. I had no strength.

[9]Then the man spoke to me! As I listened to him, I fell asleep with my face on the ground.

[10]Then he touched me! I got up on my hands and knees. I was shaking with fear. [11]He said, "Daniel! You are a man whom God likes! Stand up! Think carefully about the things that I am telling you. I have been sent to you. [14]I have come to tell you what will happen to your people in the future. This vision is about the last days."

[11:36]"A king is coming who will do anything he wants. He will make himself bigger and better than any make-believe god. He will even say terrible things about the true God! He will do whatever he wants until the time of anger is over. This is all planned. It will happen."

[11:32]"In those days, the king will talk people into turning away from God's holy covenant. But the people who know their God will be strong and will do the right things. [33]Wise people will teach many others. Many will be killed with swords, with fire, in prison, and in war. [45b]But the king will come to his own end. No one will help him."

[12:1]"At that time, Michael will come. (Michael is the great prince. He is the angel who protects your people.) It will be a terrible time. It will be the most terrible time ever! But at that time, your people will be saved! Everyone whose name is **written in God's book** will be saved! [2]All the dead people (people who "sleep" in the ground) will come back to life. Some will live forever with God. The others will be punished forever. [3]Wise people will shine like the sky! People who taught others to live the right way will shine like the stars forever and ever!"

In Your Words

1. Daniel got a message from God. What was it about?

2. Daniel saw a vision that explained the message. Who talked to Daniel in the vision?

3. Daniel learned that some people will live forever with God. How can you live forever with God?

Changes Between the Testaments

The Bible is divided into two parts called testaments. Our first forty-seven readings were from the first part, the Old Testament. In Old Testament times, the people of Israel were called Israelites. They ruled their own land with judges and with kings. They spoke and wrote in a language called Hebrew. Near the end of this time, the Israelites were taken from their land. When they came back, they no longer ruled their own land. The Persians were their rulers. They now spoke and wrote in a language called Aramaic.

There are thirty-nine books in the Old Testament. Most are written in Hebrew. Parts of the books Ezra, Daniel, and Jeremiah are written in Aramaic.

The second part of the Bible is called the New Testament. Between Old and New Testament times, many things happened. A man named Alexander from Greece took over the whole world. He made all the people in the world speak his language: Greek. Just before the start of New Testament times, another nation took over the world. From the country of Italy and the city of Rome, the Romans became the new rulers of the world.

In New Testament times, the people of Israel were called Jews. They lived in the same land, but were ruled by Roman governors. They could speak and write in three languages: Hebrew, Aramaic, and Greek. In the Old Testament God's special name is Yahweh. In the New Testament there is no Greek word for Yahweh. The Jewish people called him Lord.

There are twenty-seven books in the New Testament. All of them are written in Greek. Our next twenty-five readings come from the New Testament.

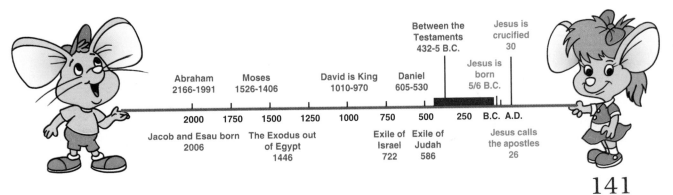

Abraham 2166-1991 | Moses 1526-1406 | David is King 1010-970 | Daniel 605-530 | Between the Testaments 432-5 B.C. | Jesus is born 5/6 B.C. | Jesus is crucified 30

2000 1750 1500 1250 1000 750 500 250 B.C. A.D.

Jacob and Esau born 2006 | The Exodus out of Egypt 1446 | Exile of Israel 722 | Exile of Judah 586 | Jesus calls the apostles 26

Have you ever answered the phone and heard the voice of your best friend? Maybe your best friend told you, "Yes, my mom said I can come to your house today!" That was good news. Have you ever opened the mailbox and found a letter with your name on it? You quickly opened it and saw that it was a birthday card from your aunt or uncle. That was joyful news.

Once some shepherds got a message from an **angel**. The angel told them about the birth of **Messiah**, the Lord. That message was good news. It was joyful news for all the people!

In Other Words

Angels are special servants of God. Sometimes God sends angels from heaven with special messages for his people. Angels look like people but they are not people.

Glory is something we can see about our God who we cannot see. Before God made the sun, moon, and stars there was light. That shiny light was probably God's glory. In the new Jerusalem there won't be a sun, a moon, or stars. Jesus will be the city's lamp! His glory will light up the city.

manger. A manger is a feeding box for animals. You slept in a crib when you were a baby. Jesus slept in a manger!

Messiah means an "anointed one." (Remember when Samuel anointed David?) The Jews were waiting for a special person to come to them from God. The baby Jesus is that special person. He is the Messiah, the Lord.

In God's Words
Luke 2:1-20

¹These things happened when Jesus was due to be born. The ruler of the world, Caesar Augustus, ordered every country in the world to make a list of all their people. ³Everyone went to the towns where they were born so their names could be written on the list.

⁴A man named Joseph went up from the town of Nazareth in Galilee. He went to Judea, to Bethlehem the town of David. Joseph did this because he was from David's family. ⁵Joseph went with Mary. Mary was engaged to be married to Joseph. She was pregnant. ⁶While they were in Bethlehem, the time came for the baby to be born. ⁷Mary's firstborn child was a son. She wrapped him in cloths and placed him in a **manger**. They were staying with

the animals because there was no room for them in the inn.

[8]Some shepherds were nearby. They were living out in the fields to watch over their flocks at night. [9]An angel of the Lord appeared to them! The **glory** of the Lord was shining around them. They were very scared. [10]But the angel said to them, "Do not be scared. I bring you good news, joyful news for all the people. [11]Today, in the town of David, your Savior has been born! He is the Messiah, the Lord. [12]This is how you will know him: You will find the baby wrapped in cloths and lying in a manger."

[13]Suddenly many more angels from heaven were with the angel of the Lord. They were all praising God and saying,

[14]"Glory to God in heaven above!
Peace to people on earth—to people with whom God is pleased!"

[15]Then the angels left them and went back to heaven. The shepherds said to each other, "Let's go to Bethlehem! Let's see this thing that the Lord has told us about!" [16]So they ran and found Mary and Joseph and the baby. The baby was lying in the manger. [17]The shepherds saw the baby. They told everyone what the angel told them about the child. [18]Everyone was amazed when they heard what the shepherds said. [19]But Mary kept all these things to herself. She thought about them in her heart. [20]Then the shepherds went back to the fields. They gave glory and praise to God for all the things they heard and saw. Everything happened just as the angel told them.

In Your Words

1. How did the shepherds know the Messiah when they saw him?

2. Why did the shepherds give glory and praise to God for all the things they heard and saw?

3. The angel told the shepherds the good news, the joyful news. Not everyone has been told the good and joyful news. Who will you tell? What will you tell them?

144

49

The Boy Jesus in His Father's House

Jesus is amazing his mother again! She was surprised when the shepherds told her the angel's message about her baby, Jesus. They said he was the Messiah, the Lord! Now she is surprised that her twelve-year-old son is talking with the **teachers**. She is surprised at the things Jesus' **Father** wants him to do. But one thing doesn't surprise her. She knows that her son, Jesus, will obey her all of the time.

In Other Words

Father. When Jesus talks about his Father, he is talking about God, not Joseph.

Feast of Passover. This is one of three feasts the Jews came to Jerusalem to celebrate each year. It helped them remember the strong way God freed them from their slavery in Egypt.

teachers. These men knew all about the Bible. They would help people understand what the Bible said. Today people go to court when they can't solve a problem with another person. In Bible times, the people went to the teachers. The teachers helped them solve their problems with each other.

The **temple** was God's house. It was a special place where God showed his glory.

In God's Words
Luke 2:41-52

[41]Every year Jesus' parents went to Jerusalem for the **Feast of Passover**. [42]When Jesus was twelve years old, they went up to the Feast as they usually did. [43]After the Feast was over, Jesus' parents started home. But the boy Jesus stayed behind in Jerusalem. Jesus' parents did not know this. [44]His parents thought Jesus was with their group. The group traveled for a whole day. Then Jesus' parents started looking for him among their family and friends. [45]They did not find him. So they went back to Jerusalem to look for Jesus.

[46]Three days later they found him. Jesus was in the **temple**, sitting among the teachers. He was listening to the teachers and even asking them questions. [47]Everyone who heard Jesus was amazed. He knew so much and he answered so well!

[48]When his parents saw him, they could not believe it! Jesus' mother said to him, "Son, why did you do this to us? Your father and I were very worried. We looked everywhere for you."

[49]Jesus said, "Why were you looking for me? You should know that I must be where my Father wants me!" [50]But his parents did not understand what Jesus meant.

[51]Then Jesus went back to Nazareth with them. He obeyed his parents all the time. But his mother kept thinking about all these things in her heart. [52]Jesus grew wiser, and grew taller, and grew to please God and people more and more.

In Your Words

1. How often did Jesus obey his parents?

2. Why were the people amazed as they listened to Jesus talk with the teachers? Why do you think Jesus knew so much about God and the Bible?

3. Jesus grew taller and taller. You're growing taller and taller, too! Jesus also grew to please God and people more and more. What can you do to please God and people more and more each day?

50

John the Baptist Tells about Jesus

Imagine building a long road to a special place. It has to pass through deep valleys. The road has to climb over tall mountains. It even has to stretch across rocky places. You would need all sorts of equipment to build a road like this.

John the Baptist is going to make a road ready for Jesus. He's not going to smooth rocky places with a powerful machine. He's not going to build steel bridges to cross deep valleys. He's going to **baptize** people who say they are sorry they have sinned against God. That's how he's going to make the road ready for Jesus. Now the people can come to Jesus without stumbling over their sins.

In Other Words

John **baptized** people by carefully dunking them in the Jordan River. To be baptized was to do something unusal. It showed that people were different. It showed that they were part of John's group. Even Jesus was baptized. He wanted to show others that he was part of this new group of people who pleased God.

Christ is not Jesus' last name! It is his title. It means "anointed one." Just like Samuel anointed David to be the king of Israel, God anointed Jesus to be the king of the world. "Christ" is the same as the word "Messiah."

In God's Words
Mark 1:1-18

¹This is the beginning of the good news about Jesus **Christ**, the Son of God.

²Isaiah the prophet wrote:

"I will send my messenger ahead of you.
    He will make the road ready for you."
³"Someone is shouting in the desert,
'Make the road ready for the Lord!
    Make the paths smooth and straight for him!'"

⁴And so a man named John came. He baptized out in the desert. He told people to be baptized to show they were sorry they had sinned against God. He told the people God would forgive them. ⁵All sorts of people from the land of Judea and from the city of Jerusalem went out to John. They said they were sorry that they had sinned against God. John baptized them in the Jordan River. ⁶John wore a robe made of camel's hair with a leather belt around his waist. He ate grasshoppers and wild honey.

⁷This is what John said: "Someone else is coming soon. He is stronger than me. He is so much greater than me that I am not even good enough to untie his shoes. ⁸I baptize you with water, but he will baptize you with the Holy Spirit."

⁹At that time Jesus came from Nazareth in Galilee. John baptized Jesus in the Jordan River. ¹⁰When Jesus came up out of the water, he saw heaven open up. He saw the Holy Spirit come down on him like a dove. ¹¹A voice from heaven said: "You are my Son. I love you. I am very pleased with you."

¹²Right away the Spirit sent Jesus out into the desert. ¹³Jesus stayed in the desert for forty days. Satan tried to get Jesus to do something wrong. Wild animals were also there with Jesus, and the angels took care of him.

149

¹⁴Later, John was put in prison. Then Jesus went into Galilee and told people the good news of God. ¹⁵He said, "The time has come. The kingdom of God is near. Stop sinning against God. Believe the good news!"

¹⁶One day Jesus was walking beside the Sea of Galilee. He saw Simon and his brother Andrew throwing a fishing net into the Sea. (They were fishermen.) ¹⁷Jesus said, "Come, follow me! I will make you fish for people." ¹⁸Right away they left their nets and followed Jesus.

In Your Words

1. Where did John baptize the people?

2. Jesus stayed in the desert for forty days. Angels and wild animals were with him. When was another time that angels and animals were in a story about Jesus?

3. John ate different food. He ate grasshoppers and wild honey! John wore different clothes. He wore a robe made of camel's hair. But he pleased God. It's not what we eat that matters. And it's not how we dress that's important. What's most important is what we say and what we do. The things we do and say show others that we please God. What will you do this week that pleases God?

51
What Blessed People Are Like

Once Moses was on Mount Sinai. Yahweh came down in a cloud and stood there with Moses. Yahweh told Moses about himself. He told Moses a list describing what he is like. Another time, Isaiah the prophet told the people what Jesus would be like. He gave them a list too. Now, Jesus is going to teach the people. And he is going to give them a list describing what God wants them to be like.

In Other Words

Disciples are people who follow Jesus—like Peter and James in the last reading, and like you and me today!

poor in spirit. People who know that they have nothing to offer God are poor in spirit. They know they are helpless without God.

People who **mourn** are people who are sad that they sin against God. They are sad that other people sin against God, too. They ask God to forgive them.

People who show **mercy** are good and kind. They are good and kind to people who are hurting or in trouble.

People who are pure in heart don't try to lie to God. They love God more than anything!

In God's Words
Matthew 5:1-12

¹Jesus saw lots of people following him in Galilee. He went up on a hill and sat down. His **disciples** came to him. ²Jesus began to teach the people. He said:

³"God blesses people who are **poor in spirit**.
   The kingdom of heaven belongs to them.
⁴God blesses people who **mourn**.
   God and other people will comfort them and make them feel
      better.
⁵God blesses people who are quiet and gentle.
   The earth will belong to them.
⁶God blesses people who are hungry and thirsty to do right.
   They will be filled up.
⁷God blesses people who show **mercy**.
   God and other people will show mercy to them.
⁸God blesses people who are the pure in heart.
   They will see God.
⁹God blesses people who make peace.
   They will be called the children of God.
¹⁰God blesses people who are treated badly because they do right.
   The kingdom of heaven belongs to them.

¹¹"God blesses you when people call you bad names and when they treat you badly. God blesses you when people lie and say all kinds of bad things against you because of Jesus. ¹²Be happy and be glad! Because your reward in heaven is very great! Remember that people also treated the prophets very badly long before you were born."

In Your Words

1. What kind of people will be called the children of God?

2. How do you show mercy to other people? To whom can you show mercy?

3. What will you be like if you are pure in heart?

152

52

Jesus Teaches about Prayer

If you wanted to learn how to jump rope, who would you ask to teach you? I would probably ask a skilled rope jumper. If you wanted to learn how to shoot a basketball, who would you ask to teach you? Maybe you would ask someone who swishes the basketball through the hoop over and over again. Jesus' disciples want to know how to pray. Who do you think they will ask to teach them? Jesus will teach them! They've watched him pray. Now they will learn how to pray.

In Other Words

God's name is holy. When people obey him, and pray to him, and praise him, they **treat his name as holy**.

When we obey God, then his **will is done**.

The **evil one** is Satan, the devil. He wants to tempt us to sin against God.

In God's Words
Matthew 6:9-13

9Jesus said, "This is the way you should pray:

" 'Our Father in heaven,
Let your name be **treated as holy**.
10Let your kingdom come.
    Let your **will be done** on earth as it is in heaven.
11Give us our daily bread each day.
12Forgive us when we do wrong against you,

for we forgive everyone who does wrong against us.
¹³Do not let us be tempted to do evil things,
but save us from the **evil one**.' "

Luke 11:5-13

⁵Then Jesus said to the people, "Let's say one of you has a friend. And let's say you go to your friend at midnight and say, 'Friend, lend me three loaves of bread. ⁶A friend of mine has come to visit me, and I have nothing to feed him.'

⁷"Your friend would probably say, 'Don't bother me! The door is already locked! I am in bed and so are my children! I can't get up and give you anything.' ⁸I tell you, your friend might not get up and give you the bread because he is your friend. But if you keep asking he will get up and give you whatever you want.

⁹"So I say to you: Ask and it will be given to you. Look and you will find. Knock and the door will be opened to you. ¹⁰For everyone who asks receives. Everyone who looks finds. And everyone who knocks gets the door opened.

[11]"Now listen, you fathers: If your son asks for a fish, do you give him a snake instead? [12]If your son asks for an egg, do you give him a scorpion? [13]You evil fathers know how to give good gifts to your children. Just think how much more your Father in heaven will give the Holy Spirit to those who ask him!"

In Your Words

1. God's will is done in heaven. Where else should we ask God to have his will done? What can you do to make sure God's will is done on earth?

2. Did the man give his friend bread because he was his friend? Or did he give his friend bread because he kept asking? What is Jesus' story telling the disciples about praying?

3. What will you do to treat God's name as holy?

53

Little Children and a Rich Man

If you rub your chewing gum in your classmate's hair, you're being childish. If you complain and cry because you can't stay up later than your usual bedtime, you are being childish, too. But when you trust your mom to feed and care for you, you're being childlike. When you sit still and trust your dad to remove a splinter from your throbbing finger, you're being childlike too.

God doesn't want his people to be childish. But he wants them to be childlike. Sometimes it's difficult for grown-ups to be childlike. It's easier for you. So trust him to love and protect you. Be childlike for him. Come to him. That's what he wants you to do.

In Other Words

eternal life. People who believe in Jesus enter the kingdom of God. They are "born again." They live forever.

In God's Words
Mark 10:13-27

[13]People were bringing their little children to Jesus so that he would touch the children. But the disciples scolded the people. [14]When Jesus saw this, he became angry. He said to the disciples, "Let the little children come to me. Do not stop them. The kingdom of God belongs to people who are like little children. [15]I tell you the truth: People must accept the kingdom of God like a little child does. If they do not, they will never enter the kingdom." [16]Then Jesus gathered the little children in his arms. He put his hands on them and he blessed them.

[17]Jesus started to walk down the road. A man ran up and got down on his knees in front of Jesus. He asked, "Good teacher, what must I do so that I may have **eternal life**?"

[18]Jesus said to him, "Why do you call me 'good'? No person is really good. Only God is good. [19]You know God's commandments, don't you? 'You must never murder. You must never commit adultery. You must never steal. You must never tell lies about your neighbor. You must never cheat anyone. Honor your father and your mother.' "

[20]The man said, "Teacher, I have done all these things since I was a little boy."

[21]Jesus looked at the young man and he felt love for him. He said, "There is one more thing you need to do. Sell all the things you own and give the money to the poor. Then you will have your treasure in heaven. And then

157

come and follow me."

²²When the man heard this, he was surprised. He went away very sad, because he owned many, many things.

²³Jesus looked around and said to his disciples, "How hard it is for rich people to enter the kingdom of God!"

²⁴The disciples were surprised by what he said. But Jesus said again, "Children, how hard it is to enter the kingdom of God! ²⁵It is easier for a camel to go through the eye of a needle than for a rich person to enter the kingdom of God."

²⁶Now the disciples were really surprised! They said to each other, "Who in the world can be saved?"

²⁷Jesus looked at them and said, "It is impossible for people to save themselves. Only God can save them."

In Your Words

1. What will people be like who will receive the kingdom of God?

2. When you're acting childish, you're doing what's bad about being a child. You're being selfish, whining, and complaining. List five things that you think are childish.

3. When you're acting childlike, you're doing what's good about being a child. You're trusting, honest and depending on someone else to help you. List five things that you think are childlike.

54
Jesus Raises a Girl from the Dead

When members of our family die, we are sad. If friends die, we are sad, too. Usually we cry. Other people around us cry. We are sad because we can't talk to them again. We cry because we won't be able to go places with them anymore. We miss them.

People who believe that Jesus died for their sins may die. But Jesus will bring them back to life one day. Jesus raised a few people from the dead while he lived on earth. One day he will raise many people from the dead. And best of all, one day there won't be any more death! There won't be any more crying. There won't be any more pain. Jesus promised. And remember, Jesus always keeps his promises.

In Other Words

A **synagogue** is a building where Jewish people meet to study the Bible and pray to God. It is like a Jewish church.

When people die, their body stays on earth but their spirit goes to God. When Jesus raised Jairus's daughter from the dead, her **spirit came back** into her body. She was alive again!

In God's Words
Luke 8:40-42;49-56

40Jesus came back to Galilee. A crowd of people welcomed him. They were all looking for him. 41A man named Jairus was a leader of the **synagogue**. He came and fell to the ground at Jesus' feet. He begged Jesus to come to his house. 42Jairus had a twelve-year-old daughter, his only daughter, and she was dying.

Jesus started to go but the people crowded all around him. 49Then someone came from the house of Jairus, the leader of the synagogue. He said, "Your daughter is dead. Don't bother the teacher any more."

159

[50]But when Jesus heard this, he said to Jairus, "Don't be afraid! Just believe, and your daughter will get better."

[51]Jesus came to Jairus's house. He let his disciples Peter, John, and James come in with him. He also let the girl's father and mother come in. He did not let anyone else inside. [52]All the people stayed outside, crying and mourning for the girl. Jesus said, "Stop your crying! She is not dead. She is only asleep."

[53]The people laughed at Jesus. They knew that the girl was dead. [54]But Jesus held her hand and said, "My child, get up!" [55]Her **spirit came back** and she stood right up! Jesus told the people to give her something to eat. [56]The girl's parents were very surprised. But Jesus ordered them not to tell anyone what had happened.

In Your Words

1. Who was Jairus?

2. What did Jesus want Jairus to believe?

3. Jesus told the girl's parents not to tell others what he did. He told them not to tell because he didn't want people to come to him like he was a magician in a circus. He wanted people to come to him and listen to what he told them about God. He wanted people to learn how to do things that pleased God. When you read about the miracles Jesus did, praise God. Then knowing his power, trust him to help you do things he wants you to do.

55

Jesus Feeds Five Thousand People

Once Jesus was in a boat with his disciples. The wind blew the boat. The waves crashed against the boat. The disciples were afraid. Jesus told the wind to stop. He told the waves to be still. The wind and waves did what he said. The wind stopped. The waters became quiet. Next to that same lake, Jesus saw some people following him. He felt sorry for them. He said that they were like sheep without a shepherd. He had them lie down on the green grass—all five thousand of them!

Jesus is acting like the good shepherd David told us about in Psalm 23. Jesus is having the people lie down in soft, green grass next to quiet waters. He is doing what Yahweh did. Imagine that! Now he's going to feed all the people. He's going to feed them all with five loaves of bread and two small fish. How can he do that? Jesus is very powerful. He's powerful just like Yahweh.

In Other Words

A **miracle** is a sign from God. When Jesus healed the sick or gave sight to the blind or raised people from the dead, he showed he was from God. The greatest miracle was when Jesus was raised from the dead.

In God's Words
John 6:1-14

[1]Some time later, Jesus went to the other side of the Sea of Galilee. (This sea is also called the Sea of Tiberias.) [2]Many people followed him because they saw Jesus heal sick people with miracles. [3]Jesus went up on a hill and sat down with his disciples. [4]It was almost time for the Jewish Passover Feast. [5]Jesus looked up and saw many people coming to him. He said to Philip, "Where can we buy bread for these people to eat?" [6]Jesus asked this to test Philip. Jesus already knew what he was going to do.

Jesus Feeds Five Thousand People

⁷Philip said to Jesus, "Even if I worked for a year I could not buy enough bread for these people. They would not even get one bite each!"

⁸Andrew, Simon Peter's brother, was another of Jesus' disciples. He said ⁹"Here is a little boy with five loaves of barley bread and two small fish. But how can these feed so many people?"

¹⁰Jesus said, "Tell the people to sit down." There was lots of grass in that place. About five thousand men sat down. ¹¹Jesus then took the loaves of bread and gave thanks for them. Then he passed out the bread to the people who were sitting. Everyone got as much as they wanted! Jesus did the same thing with the fish.

¹²Everyone ate until they were full. Then Jesus said to his disciples, "Pick up the pieces that are left over. Don't throw anything away." ¹³So the disciples picked up the leftover pieces. The people who ate the five loaves of barley bread left enough pieces to fill up twelve whole baskets!

¹⁴The people saw that Jesus had done a **miracle**. They said, "This man *must* be the prophet who was supposed to come into the world!"

In Your Words

1. Why did many people follow Jesus at the Sea of Galilee?

2. Someone in the big crowd had some food. Who had the food? What food did he have?

3. Why did the people say, "This man *must* be the prophet who was supposed to come into the world?" How do you feel when you read about miracles Jesus did?

56
A Lost Son Comes Home

Jesus taught people many things. Sometimes he told people what he wanted them to know. Remember Jesus telling the disciples how to pray? Remember him telling them what blessed people are like? Other times Jesus taught people by telling stories. The stories were easy to understand. But each story had a hidden message. In this reading, you're going to read about a father, two sons, and some pigs. You'll understand the story. But will you discover the hidden message? Here's a hint. The father is like God. The younger son is like you and me. Now read the story. I'll ask you later about the hidden message.

In Other Words

A **famine** is when there is no food to eat.

In God's Words
Luke 15:11-24

[11]Jesus said, "Once there was a man who had two sons. [12]The younger son said to his father, 'Father, give me my share of what our family owns.' So the man gave each son his share of what the family owned.

[13]"A few days later, the younger son gathered up everything he owned. He went off to a land far away. There he lived like a fool and spent all his money. [14]After he spent all his money, there was a very bad **famine** all over the land. The young son did not have enough to eat. [15]So he got a job working for a man who lived in that land. The man sent him to his fields to feed pigs. [16]The young son was so hungry, he wanted to eat with the pigs! But no one gave him anything to eat.

[17]"Then he started thinking rightly. He said, 'All the men who work for my father have plenty of bread. But I am dying of hunger here in this famine! [18]I will get up and go back to my father. I will say to him: Father, I have sinned against God in heaven and

against you. ¹⁹I am not good enough to be called your son any more. Just give me a job like one of your workers.' ²⁰So he got up and went back to his father.

"While the young son was still far away, his father saw him. He felt love and kindness for his son. He ran out to his son and hugged him and kissed him.

²¹"The son said to him, 'Father, I have sinned against God in heaven and against you. I am not good enough to be called your son any more.'

²²"But the father called his servants. He said, 'Hurry! Bring the best robe and put it on my son. Put a ring on his finger. Put shoes on his feet. ²³Bring the fat calf and kill it. Let's eat and have a great time! ²⁴For my son was dead, but now he is alive again. He was lost, but now he is found.' So they had a great time."

In Your Words

1. Did you discover the hidden message? If God is like the father in the story, what will he do when we come back to him after we sin?

2. If we are like the younger son, what should we do when we sin?

3. The younger son said to his father, "I have sinned against God in heaven and against you. I am not good enough to be called your son any more." Sometimes we will sin against our Father in heaven, too. When we do, we can come back to him. We can return just as the younger son returned. Read 1 John 1:9 in a Bible. It's a promise from God. Remember it. Think rightly just as the younger son learned to think rightly. Read 1 John 1:9 and do what it says.

57
Zacchaeus: The Littlest Disciple

Have you ever been in a crowd of people? Maybe a famous person was coming your way. You wanted to see that person, but you weren't tall enough. You couldn't see the famous person's face. All you could see were people's knees and their shiny belt buckles. If your mom or dad was there, they probably lifted you up. When you got up high, you could see the famous person.

Once Jesus came to a city. Many people came out to see him. They crowded around him. A small man wanted to see Jesus, too. But he couldn't see Jesus. He could see only the people in the crowd. He didn't have a dad to lift him up, so he climbed a tree. From that tree he saw Jesus and Jesus saw him. Then Jesus told the small man some most amazing things.

In Other Words

Tax collectors collected money that people had to pay to the leaders of their country. Sometimes the tax collectors made the people pay *more* money than they had to! That is why some tax collectors were rich. That is why people hated tax collectors. That is why they called them sinful.

In God's Words
Luke 19:1-10

[1]Jesus came to Jericho and went through the city. [2]A man named Zacchaeus lived there. He was an important **tax collector**. He was very rich. [3]He wanted to see who Jesus was. But Zacchaeus was a short man—he could not see Jesus because of all the people. [4]He saw where Jesus was going and he ran ahead of him. He climbed up a sycamore tree so he could see Jesus.

[5]When Jesus came to the tree, he looked up and said, "Zacchaeus, come down right now! I want to stay at your house today." [6]So Zacchaeus came right down! He was very happy to have Jesus in his home.

[7]All the people saw this and they complained. They said, "Jesus is staying in the house of a sinful man."

[8]Zacchaeus stood up and said to the Lord, "Look, here is half of everything I own. Lord, I will give this to the poor. If I have taken too much money from anyone, I will pay back four times more than I took."

[9]Jesus said to him, "Today salvation has come to this house. This man really is a son of Abraham. [10]For the Son of Man came to look for lost people and to save them."

In Your Words

1. Where was Zacchaeus when he finally got to see Jesus? Why was he up there?

2. Why did the people complain when they found out that Jesus was going to stay at Zacchaeus's house?

3. We don't have to climb trees to see Jesus. We can read all about him in the amazing book, the Bible. What are some things you've learned about Jesus? Tell others what you have learned.

58

King Jesus Comes to Jerusalem

When Jesus was twelve years old, his parents found him in the temple. He was sitting among the teachers. Everyone was amazed at the things the boy Jesus said. He was so young, but he knew so much. He answered so well!

Now Jesus is in the temple again. This time the people are amazed at the things he does. He is doing wonderful miracles. He is doing things the prophets said the Messiah would do. He is not the boy Jesus anymore. He is the king Jesus. Many of the grown-ups are mad at him. But the children, even little babies, are praising him!

In Other Words

Cloaks are like coats. People wore cloaks when the weather was cool. John the Baptist had a cloak made from camel's hair.

Daughter Zion. Zion is a name for the city of Jerusalem, God's favorite city where his temple was built. He calls Zion his daughter because the city is so important to him.

Hosanna is a Hebrew word. It means "save us, please!"

A **lame** person cannot walk. Jesus made the lame walk. He made the blind see.

In God's Words
Matthew 21:1-16

[1]Jesus and his disciples came near to Jerusalem. They came to the village of Bethphage on the Mount of Olives. Jesus sent away two disciples. [2]He said to them, "Go to the village ahead of you. Right away you will find a donkey there. She will be tied to a post next to her colt. Untie them and bring them to me. [3]If any man says anything to you, tell him that the Lord needs these animals. Then the man will send the animals right away."

⁴Jesus did this so that the words the prophet spoke would come true:

⁵"Say to the **Daughter Zion**,
 'Look, your king is coming to you!
He is gentle and is riding on a donkey.
 He is riding on a colt, on a baby donkey.' "

⁶The disciples went and did just as Jesus told them. ⁷They brought back the donkey and the colt. They placed their **cloaks** on the animals. And Jesus sat on top of the cloaks. ⁸A large crowd of people put their cloaks on the road in front of Jesus. Other people cut branches from the trees and put them on the road. ⁹Many people went ahead of Jesus and others followed him. They all shouted,

"**Hosanna** to the Son of David!"
"May God bless the man who comes in the name of the Lord!"
"Hosanna in the highest heaven!"

¹⁰When Jesus came into Jerusalem, the whole city was excited. People asked, "Who is this?"

¹¹The crowds said, "This is Jesus. He is the prophet from Nazareth in Galilee."

¹²Jesus went into the temple area. Some people were buying and selling things there. Jesus made them go away. Some people were trading Jewish money for money from other countries. Jesus turned their tables upside down. Other people were selling doves for sacrifices. Jesus knocked their chairs over. ¹³Jesus said to these people, "God says in the Bible, 'My house will be called a house of prayer.' But you people are making God's house a 'den of robbers.' "

¹⁴Blind people and **lame** people came to Jesus at the temple. Jesus healed them. ¹⁵The chief priests and the teachers of the law saw the wonderful miracles Jesus did. They heard the children shouting in the temple area, "Hosanna to the Son of David." The priests and the teachers were very upset.

¹⁶They asked Jesus, "Do you hear what these children are saying?"

Jesus said to them, "Yes! Haven't you ever read in the Bible, 'God brings praise from the mouths of children and little babies'?"

In Your Words

1. Remember how John the Baptist prepared the way for Jesus? He asked people to repent and be baptized. Now the people are preparing the path for Jesus. What are they throwing on the ground to make his path smooth?

2. Read Zechariah 9:9 in a Bible. Then think about this story. Jesus is the king to come. The people expected him to come. Now he is here. Do you think they will ever believe that he is Messiah the Lord? Do you believe that Jesus is Messiah the Lord?

3. Praise is telling others what God is like and what he has done. Children and little babies praised God when Jesus entered the city on the donkey. Now it's your turn to praise God. Think of what God is like. Remember something God has done. Now go and tell someone else about God. Praise him!

59

The Greatest Son and the Greatest Commandment

Once the **Pharisees** asked Jesus a difficult question. He answered them. He told them the greatest commandment. Later, Jesus asked the Pharisees an easy question. They wouldn't answer him. They knew the right answer, but they didn't want to say it. They didn't want to admit that Jesus was greater than David. They didn't want to admit that Jesus was the **Messiah**. But Jesus is greater than David. And Jesus is the Messiah. Only Jesus is the son of David and the son of God. There is no one else like Jesus!

In Other Words

The Law and the Prophets were the two largest parts of the Jewish Bible. Christians call these books the Old Testament.

Messiah means "anointed." The Jewish people were waiting for God to send the Messiah to save them from their enemies. They did not understand that God wanted the Messiah to save them from their sins. They did not understand that Jesus was the Messiah, the Christ, the son of David, the son of God.

Pharisees were leaders of the Jewish people. The people thought the Pharisees were very important and godly people. But Jesus said that the Pharisees wanted to please people more than they wanted to please God. The Pharisees did not like Jesus.

In God's Words
Matthew 22:34b-46

[34b]Some of the Pharisees came together. [35]One of them knew the law very well. He asked a question to test Jesus. [36]"Teacher, what is the greatest commandment in the law?" [37]Jesus said to him, " 'You

must love the Lord your God with all your heart, and with all your soul, and with all your mind.' [38]This is the greatest commandment. This is the first commandment. [39]The second commandment is like it: 'You must love your neighbor as you love yourself.' [40]Everything in **the Law and the Prophets** depends on these two commandments."

[41]The Pharisees were still gathered together. Jesus asked them, [42]"What do you think about the Messiah? Whose son is he?"

The Pharisees said, "He is the son of David."

[43]Jesus said to them, "David spoke about the Messiah by the power of the Holy Spirit. David called him 'Lord.' How could he do that? David said,

[44]" 'The Lord said to my Lord:
"Sit at my right hand.
I will make your enemies
   bow down at your feet." '

[45]"If David calls the Messiah 'Lord,' how can he be David's son?" [46]None of the Pharisees could say a word to Jesus. From that day on none of them dared to ask Jesus any more questions.

In Your Words

1. Do you remember reading about the greatest commandment already? (Look back at reading 23.) Now would be a very good time to memorize Deuteronomy 6:4-5.

2. Whose son is the Messiah? What did David call the Messiah?

3. How can the Messiah be David's son and David's Lord at the same time?

60
Jesus Makes the New Covenant

When Jesus came into Jerusalem on the little donkey, everything happened just as Zechariah the prophet said it would happen. Now Jesus is sending Peter and John on an errand. He's telling them where to go. He's telling them what to do. But he's also telling them things that will happen. He's telling them things that will happen before they even happen! Can you believe it? And guess what. Everything happened just as Jesus said it would happen. Do you think Peter and John were amazed? Jesus is not an ordinary man.

In Other Words

Jesus chose twelve **apostles** to learn about him. Then he sent them to tell the whole world about Jesus, the Holy Spirit, and the kingdom of God.

new covenant. God made a covenant with Israel at Mount Sinai. The Ten Commandments were part of that covenant (reading 24). Israel promised to do everything that God told them. But they did not obey God. They broke the covenant. So God made a new covenant with all people. He sent his son Jesus to die for our sins and to come back to life again. If you believe in Jesus you have eternal life. You are part of God's new covenant.

Son of Man means "human being." It also is a special, secret name for the Messiah. Jesus liked to call himself the Son of Man. His disciples knew that meant he was the Messiah. We know that, too.

In God's Words
Luke 22:7-23

⁷Then the Day of Unleavened Bread came. (This was the day the people sacrificed the Passover lamb.) ⁸Jesus sent Peter and John on an errand. He said, "Go and get everything ready for Passover. Then we can eat the Passover dinner."

Jesus Makes the New Covenant

[9]Peter and John asked Jesus, "Where do you want us to get things ready?"

[10]Jesus said to them, "First, go into the city. There you will meet a man carrying a jar of water. Follow him until he goes into a house. [11]Then talk to the man who owns the house. Say, 'The Teacher says, "Do you have a guest room? May I eat the Passover dinner there with my disciples?" ' [12]That man will take you upstairs and show you a large room. The room will be all ready for you. Get everything ready for dinner in that room."

[13]So Peter and John left. Everything happened just as Jesus said it would. They got everything ready for the Passover dinner.

[14]When it was time, Jesus and his **apostles** sat around the table. [15]Jesus said to them, "I want very much to eat this Passover dinner with you. Soon I will suffer. [16]I tell you, I will not eat the Passover dinner again until the kingdom of God comes. Then people will see the true meaning of the Passover."

[17]Jesus took a cup of wine. He thanked God for it and said, "Take this cup. All of you drink from it. [18]I tell you, I will not drink wine again until the kingdom of God comes."

[19]Then Jesus took bread and thanked God for it. He broke the bread into pieces and gave it to his disciples. He said, "This is my body which I give for you. Eat this bread to remember me."

[20]Jesus did this the same way after dinner. He took a cup of wine and said, "This cup is the **new covenant** in my blood. My blood is poured out for you. [21]But someone here at the table will turn against me. [22]Everything that God has planned will happen to the **Son of Man**. But the man who turns against the Son of Man will still be punished!" [23]Then the disciples began to talk to each other. They wondered which one of them would ever do such a thing.

In Your Words

1. Jesus wanted Peter and John to get things ready for a special dinner. What was that dinner called?

2. What did Jesus say that let the apostles know that he would not be with them for much longer?

3. Jesus told the apostles that his blood was poured out for them. His blood was poured out for you and me, too. Long ago Jesus died for our sins so that we wouldn't have to die for our own sins today. Do you believe that? If you believe that Jesus died for you, you have eternal life. And you are part of God's new covenant.

61
Jesus Prays in the Garden

Sometimes Jesus taught people using stories. Remember his story about a man who kept asking his friend for three loaves of bread? Remember how the man kept asking and asking? He kept asking even though it was midnight. He kept asking even though his friend's family was asleep. But the man got three loaves of bread. The man's friend gave him the three loaves of bread because he kept asking and asking. Jesus used this story to teach his disciples how to pray. The disciples learned to keep asking and asking when they prayed. Now Jesus is praying. He's asking and asking. He doesn't want to die. But he's praying just like he taught his disciples. He says to God, "Do not let my will be done. Let your will be done."

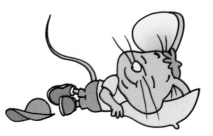

In Other Words

this cup. The cup of wine at the Passover dinner was a picture of Jesus' blood. When Jesus died for us, blood came from his wounds. This cup also pictures his death. Jesus did not want to die; he did not want to "drink this cup." But he chose to do what God the Father wanted.

In God's Words
Matthew 26:36-46

[36]Then Jesus went with his disciples to a garden called Gethsemane. Jesus said to them, "Sit here while I go over there to pray." [37]Jesus took with him Peter and the two sons of Zebedee, James and John. Jesus became sad and upset. [38]Then he said to them, "My soul is very sad—sad enough to die. Stay here and stay awake with me."

[39]Jesus went a little farther away. He knelt down with his face to the ground. He prayed, "My Father, if it can be done, let **this cup**

be taken from me. But do not let my will be done. Let your will be done."

⁴⁰Then Jesus came back to his disciples. He found them sleeping. He said to Peter, "Couldn't you all stay awake with me for one hour? ⁴¹Stay awake and pray that you will not be tempted to do wrong. Your spirit is ready to obey, but your body is weak."

⁴²Jesus went away a second time. He prayed, "My Father, if this cup cannot be taken away unless I drink it, let your will be done."

⁴³Then Jesus came back. Again he found the disciples sleeping. (They couldn't keep their eyes open.) ⁴⁴So he left them and went away again. Jesus prayed a third time. He prayed the same way as before. ⁴⁵Then he came back to the disciples. He said to them, "Are you still sleeping and resting? Look, the hour has come! The Son of Man is betrayed into the hands of sinners. ⁴⁶Get up! Let's go! Look, here comes the one who is betraying me!"

In Your Words

1. Who did Jesus take with him when he prayed?

2. Jesus prayed, "My Father, if it can be done, let this cup be taken from me. But do not let my will be done. Let your will be done." When was another time that Jesus said, "Let your will be done?" What was he teaching his disciples to do?

3. Peter, James, and John fell asleep. They fell asleep even after Jesus asked them to stay awake. They were not as strong as Jesus. They couldn't stay awake. Sometimes we can't do the things that please God. But Jesus always does what he wants to do. We are weak; he is strong. Think of something you want to do that pleases God. Ask Jesus to make you strong. Ask Jesus to make you strong so that you can do what pleases God.

62
Jesus Is Arrested in the Garden

In the first reading we pretended to make things just by saying their names. Then we read how God said the names of things and they were made. Only God can make things just by saying their names! Another time we read about God telling Moses his name. God told Moses that his name is **I AM**, his name is Yahweh. Moses told the Israelites that I AM sent him to help them. Now we are going to read about a group of soldiers and some officers. They came to Jesus in the garden. The chief priests and Pharisees came, too. Jesus asked them, "Who are you looking for?" They said, "Jesus of Nazareth." Jesus said, "I AM." The soldiers fell down because of Jesus' powerful name. But Jesus did not save himself. He chose to obey his Father.

In Other Words

betrayed. Judas was a member of Jesus' group. But Judas told Jesus' enemies where they could find Jesus. He betrayed Jesus. Judas was a traitor.

high priest. Priests led the Israelites in their worship of God. The high priest was the leader of the priests. He was a very important leader in Israel.

I AM. God told Moses that his name was I AM. Jesus is telling the people that his name is I AM, his name is Yahweh. Both the Father and Jesus are I AM.

In God's Words
John 18:2-13

²Judas was the one who **betrayed** Jesus. He knew the garden where Jesus was. Jesus met there with his disciples many times. ³So Judas came to the garden. He brought with him a group of soldiers and some

officers from the chief priests and Pharisees. They were carrying torches, lamps, and weapons.

⁴Jesus knew all the things that would happen to him. He went out and asked them, "Who are you looking for?"

⁵They said, "Jesus of Nazareth."

Jesus said, "I AM." (Now Judas, the one betraying Jesus, was standing with them.) ⁶When Jesus said, "I AM," they all stepped back and fell to the ground!

⁷Again Jesus asked them, "Who are you looking for?"

And they said, "Jesus of Nazareth."

⁸Jesus said, "I told you that I AM. If you are looking for me, let these men go." ⁹This happened to fulfill the word that Jesus had said: "I did not lose one of the men you gave me."

¹⁰Simon Peter had a sword. He took it and hit the **high priest's** servant. It cut off the servant's right ear. (The servant's name was Malchus.)

¹¹But Jesus told Peter, "Put your sword away! I must drink the cup the Father has given me!"

¹²Then the group of soldiers and its leader and the Jewish officers arrested Jesus. They tied him up. ¹³Next they took Jesus to Annas, the father-in-law of Caiaphas. Caiaphas was the high priest that year.

Matthew 27:1

¹Early in the morning, all the chief priests and the elders of the people decided to put Jesus to death.

In Your Words

1. Which disciple betrayed Jesus?

2. What does Jesus mean when he says, "I must drink the cup the Father has given me?"

3. Jesus knew all the things that would happen to him. He knew things that would happen before they happened! He knows all things that will happen to you. He knows things that will happen to you before they happen! Jesus knows everything. Jesus is strong. Jesus loves you. Is it safe to trust Jesus to take care of you? Why not thank him now that he loves you and takes care of you.

63

Jesus Is Crucified

A king tells other people what to do. He wears fancy clothes. He wears a golden crown. People carry things for the king. Sometimes they even carry the king in his fancy chair. Jesus is a king. He is the greatest king. But people didn't treat him like a king. Instead of a golden crown, they made him wear a crown of thorns. Instead of carrying him, they made him carry his own cross. They made him carry the cross they used to try to kill him. But they didn't kill Jesus. No one made Jesus die. He chose to die. He gave up his spirit when he finished doing what God the Father wanted him to do.

In Other Words

crucify. In the time of Jesus, the worst criminals were crucified. They were tied or nailed to a wooden **cross**, shaped like a "T" or a "+." The worst criminals hung on the cross until they died. Sometimes they starved to death. Sometimes they bled to death. Sometimes they just couldn't breathe any more. Jesus loved us so much, he died for us on a cross. He died on a cross just like the worst criminals.

Aramaic, Latin, and Greek were different languages spoken in Israel. Aramaic was the language of the Jewish people. Latin was the language of the Roman rulers and soldiers. Greek was the language that both Jewish people and Roman people understood.

In God's Words
John 18:28a; 19:4-7,16-22,25-30

[18:28a]Then the Jews led Jesus away from Caiaphas. They took him to the palace of Pilate, the Roman ruler.

[19:4]Pilate questioned Jesus. Then Pilate came out and said to the Jews, "Look, I am bringing Jesus out to you. I don't think he has done anything wrong. I want you to know that." [5]Then Jesus came out. He was wearing a crown of thorns and a purple robe that the soldiers put on him. Pilate said to the Jews, "Here is the man!"

[6]When the chief priests and their officers saw Jesus, they shouted, "**Crucify**! Crucify!"

But Pilate said, "You take him! You crucify him! I don't think he has done anything wrong."

[7]The Jews said to Pilate, "We have a law. The law says Jesus must die, because he said he is the Son of God."

[16]Then Pilate gave Jesus to the Jews so they could crucify him.

So they took Jesus. [17]Jesus had to carry his own **cross**. He went out to a place called Skull Place. (In **Aramaic** it is called Golgotha.) [18]Here they crucified Jesus. They crucified two other men with him, one on each side. Jesus was in the middle.

[19]Pilate had a sign made. It was put on the cross. The sign said, "Jesus of Nazareth, the King of the Jews." [20]Jesus was crucified near the city. So many of the Jews read this sign. The sign was written in Aramaic, **Latin, and Greek**. [21]The chief priests of the Jews said to Pilate, "Do not write 'The King of the Jews!' Write that this man *said* he was king of the Jews."

[22]Pilate said, "I have written what I wanted to write."

[25]Jesus' mother and his mother's sister stood near Jesus' cross. Mary the wife of Clopas and Mary Magdalene were

also there. [26]Jesus saw his mother. He also saw the disciple whom he loved standing by her. Jesus said to his mother, Mary, "Woman, here is your son." [27]And Jesus said to the disciple, "Here is your mother." From that time on, this disciple took care of Mary as his own mother.

[28]Then Jesus knew that all things were now finished. To fulfill the Scripture, Jesus said, "I am thirsty." [29]A jar full of sour wine vinegar was there. They took a sponge full of sour wine and put it on a hyssop branch. They lifted the sponge to Jesus' lips. [30]Jesus took the drink and said, "It is finished!" And then he bowed his head and gave up his spirit.

In Your Words

1. What did Pilate think Jesus had done wrong?

2. What was Jesus wearing when he left Pilate? Were the soldiers honoring Jesus with the crown and the robe? Or were they making fun of Jesus with the crown of thorns and the purple robe?

3. Jesus took the drink and said, "It is finished!" And then he bowed his head and gave up his spirit. Jesus did everything the Father wanted him to do. God wants us to do everything he wants us to do. He wants his will to be done on earth like it is in heaven. How can you remember to do what God wants you to do? One way is to memorize verses from the Bible. Look back at the readings about Jesus. Maybe you can memorize a verse or two from these readings to remind you to do what God wants you to do.

64
Jesus Rises from the Dead

An angel again! He's bringing a message from God to the women at Jesus' **tomb**. The shepherds were afraid when they first saw the angel. But the angel said to them, "Do not be scared. I bring you good news, joyful news for all the people." The angel told them that Jesus the Messiah would be born in Bethlehem. That news made the shepherds happy. The women at the tomb were frightened when they saw the angel, too. The angel told them, "Don't you be afraid. I know that you are looking for Jesus, who was crucified. He is not here. He has risen, just as he said he would." That news made the women happy. They ran to tell the disciples the great news.

In Other Words

A person with **authority** is powerful. He can control many things. Jesus obeyed the authority of God his Father. Now the Father has given Jesus authority over all things. We need to obey Jesus' authority as he obeyed his Father's authority.

Father, Son, and Holy Spirit. God is one. That's why he has one name. But God is three. The Father, the Son, and the Holy Spirit are God. This is a "mystery." Even grown-ups cannot understand it. We refer to God as the "Trinity." This means God is three in one.

A **tomb** is a place where someone's body is put after he dies. Jesus' tomb was a cave dug out of solid rock. A round stone—like a wheel—was rolled over the opening of the tomb. It could be rolled away to put other bodies in. But an angel rolled the stone away from Jesus' tomb. The angel rolled the stone away to show that Jesus' body was not there any more!

In God's Words

Matthew 28:1-10;16-20

¹It was the first day of the week, the day after the Sabbath. Early in the morning Mary Magdalene and the other Mary went to look at Jesus' tomb.

²Suddenly there was a great earthquake! An angel of the Lord came down from heaven and went to the tomb. He rolled the stone away and sat on it. ³The angel was as bright as lightning. His clothes were as white as snow. ⁴The guards at the tomb were afraid of the angel. They shook with fear. They fell down like dead men.

⁵But the angel said to the women, "Don't you be afraid. I know that you are looking for Jesus, who was crucified. ⁶He is not here. He has risen, just as he said he would. Come and see the place where he lay. ⁷Then hurry! Go and tell his disciples: 'Jesus has risen from the dead! Listen! He is going ahead of you to Galilee. There you will see him.' There! I have told you."

⁸So the women hurried away from the tomb. They were afraid, but they were very happy. They ran off to tell Jesus' disciples. ⁹Suddenly Jesus met them. "Hello!" he said. The women came to him. They knelt down and grabbed his feet. They worshiped him. ¹⁰Then Jesus said to them, "Do not be afraid. Go and tell my brothers to go to Galilee. There they will see me."

¹⁶So the eleven disciples went to Galilee. They went to the mountain where Jesus told them to go. ¹⁷When they saw Jesus, they worshiped him. But some were not sure what to do. ¹⁸Then Jesus came to them and said, "All **authority** in heaven and on earth has been given to me. ¹⁹Go now and make disciples of all nations. Baptize them in the name of the **Father and of the Son and of the Holy Spirit**. ²⁰Teach them to obey everything I have commanded you. And listen! I am with you always, to the very end of time."

In Your Words

1. Who were the first people Jesus met after he rose from the dead?

2. The women saw an angel. He was as bright as lightning. His clothes were as white as snow. Why do you think the angel is shiny, bright white?

3. Jesus told his disciples to listen to him. He told them, "I am with you always, to the very end of time." That made the disciples feel brave. It made them feel safe. If you believe in Jesus, you are his disciple, too. He is with you always. He is with you to the very end of time. How does that make you feel?

65
Peter Preaches about Jesus

Peter is telling everybody about Jesus. Once he wouldn't tell a girl that he knew Jesus, but now he is telling everyone! He is telling everyone that he was a **witness** of the things Jesus said and did. Jesus told his disciples to be his witnesses. Peter is fulfilling Jesus' commands. On the very same day the Holy Spirit came to make the church strong, Peter is being Jesus' witness. Peter is being very strong. He is being brave.

In Other Words

Resurrection means rising from the dead. God raised Jesus from the dead. Everyone who believes in Jesus will also be raised from the dead. They will be raised from the dead as Jesus was raised from the dead.

Witnesses are people who see something happen. Peter and the other apostles saw Jesus after his resurrection. They told people what they saw. You and I see Jesus change our lives. Like Peter and the other apostles, we are Jesus' witnesses, too. We can tell people about Jesus.

We **repent** when we stop doing wrong and then ask God to forgive us.

In God's Words
Acts 2:22-41

[22]"Men, people of Israel, listen to these words! God showed you that Jesus of Nazareth was a special man. Through Jesus, God did miracles, wonders, and signs among you. You know this is true. [23]God had a special plan he decided on long ago. This Jesus was

187

handed over to you. With the help of wicked men, you crucified him and killed him. [24]But God raised him up! God set him free from the pain of death. There was no way that death could hang on to him! [25]David spoke about Jesus:

" 'I saw the Lord. He is always before me.
   He is at my right hand. So I will never be upset.
[26]Because of this my heart is glad. My mouth sings for joy.
   Even my body lives in hope.
[27]Because you will not leave me in the tomb.
   You will not let your Holy One turn to dust.
[28]You have made known to me the paths of life!
   You will be with me and fill me with happiness!'

[29]"Brothers, let me tell you the truth about our father, David. David died and was buried. His tomb is here among us to this day. [30]But David was a prophet. He knew what God had promised him: One day, one of David's own descendants would sit on his throne. [31]David saw what would happen in the future. He spoke of the **resurrection** of the Messiah. He said that the Messiah would not be left in his tomb. His body would not turn to dust. [32]God has raised this Jesus to life. We are all witnesses. [33]Jesus has been raised to the right hand of God. He has received the Holy Spirit, as his Father promised. He has poured out what you now see and hear. [34]David did not go up to heaven. Yet David said,

" 'The Lord said to my Lord:
   "Sit at my right hand.
[35]I will make your enemies
   bow down at your feet." '

36"Now then let all Israel know this for sure: God has made this Jesus both Lord and Messiah. This is the same Jesus you crucified."

37When the people heard this, they felt pain in their hearts. They said to Peter and the other apostles, "Brothers, what can we do?"

38Peter said, "Every one of you must **repent**. Every one of you must be baptized in the name of Jesus Christ. Then your sins will be forgiven. Then you will receive the gift of the Holy Spirit. 39The promise is for you and your children. It is even for all those who are far away. The promise is for everyone who hears the word of the Lord our God."

40Peter warned the people with many more words. He told them again and again, "Save yourselves from this wicked generation." 41Those who welcomed his words were baptized. About three thousand people became disciples that day.

In Your Words

1. David saw what would happen in the future to the Messiah, Jesus. What is one thing David said would *not* happen to Jesus?

2. Peter told the people about the special plan God decided on long ago. God decided to have Jesus come to earth and die for our sins. He decided to raise Jesus from the dead. Peter wants everybody to know God's special plan. Do you understand God's special plan? Do you believe that Jesus died for you? If you believe that Jesus died in your place, thank him now. Pray to God and thank him for his special plan. Then be like Peter. Be one of Jesus' witnesses.

66

The Church Grows and Suffers

Remember the time a king became very angry with Daniel and his friends? He had some soldiers tie them up and throw them into a red hot furnace. But God sent his angel to rescue them. Now the **Sadducees** are going to treat the apostles badly. They're going to put the apostles in jail. But during the night an angel of the Lord is going to open the doors of the jail. An angel is going to rescue the apostles just like an angel rescued Daniel and his friends.

But God doesn't always rescue his people from trouble. Sometimes he lets his people suffer. The apostles are going to find that out. They're going to suffer bad things because they are Jesus' followers.

In Other Words

The **Sadducees** were an important group of Jewish leaders. They did not believe in miracles, angels, or the resurrection. But God showed the Sadducees that all these things were true!

In God's Words
Acts 5:12,14-32,40-42

[12]The apostles did many signs and miracles among the people. All the believers came together in a part of the temple called Solomon's Porch. [14]More and more men and women believed in the Lord. They joined with the other believers. [15]People brought sick people out into the streets. They laid them on beds and mats. They waited for Peter to pass by. They hoped that even Peter's shadow

might touch some of them. [16]Many came from the towns around Jerusalem. They also brought sick people. They brought people who were bothered by evil spirits. All of them were healed.

[17]The high priest and all the men with him were part of a group called the Sadducees. They decided to do something because they were filled with jealousy. [18]They arrested the apostles and put them in jail. [19]But during the night an angel of the Lord came. He opened the doors of the jail and led the apostles out. He said to them, [20]"Go, stand in the temple. Tell the people all about this new life."

[21]The apostles listened to what the angel said. Early in the morning they went into the temple and taught the people.

Then the high priest and his men came. They called together the council and all of the elders of Israel. They sent to the jail to bring the apostles. [22]The officers went to the jail, but they did not find the apostles. So the officers went back. They said, [23]"We found the jail locked up tight. The guards were standing at the doors. But when we opened the doors, we found no one inside!" [24]The captain of the temple and the chief priests heard these words. They were confused. They wondered what was going on.

[25]Then someone came and said, "Look! The men you put in jail are standing in the temple! They are teaching the people!" [26]So the captain and his officers went and brought back the apostles. They did not force the apostles to come. They were afraid of the people. The officers thought the people would throw stones and kill them.

[27]They brought the apostles back. The apostles stood in front of the council. The high priest asked them questions. [28]He said, "We warned you very strongly not to teach in this name! But look! You have filled Jerusalem with your teaching. You are trying to blame us for this man's blood and death."

[29]Peter and the other apostles said: "We must obey God rather than men! [30]The God of our fathers raised Jesus from the dead. You killed Jesus by hanging him on a wooden cross. [31]God raised this Jesus to his own right hand. God made him Ruler and Savior. He wants Israel to repent. He wants to forgive their sins. [32]We are witnesses of these things, and so is the Holy Spirit. God gives the

Holy Spirit to those who obey him."

[40]Then the council had the apostles beaten. They warned them not to speak in the name of Jesus. Then they let them go. [41]As the apostles left the council they rejoiced! They were happy that they were worthy to suffer bad things for the name of Jesus. [42]From that day on they kept going to the temple and to people's houses. They never stopped teaching and telling the good news about Christ Jesus.

In Your Words

1. Who arrested the apostles and put them in jail? Who opened the doors of the jail and led the apostles out?

2. The council told the apostles to stop telling the good news about Christ Jesus. What did the apostles do?

3. Turn to reading 51. Read Matthew 5:11-12. Do you think God is going to bless the apostles when they are treated badly? One day you may be treated badly because you love Jesus. God may rescue you. He may let you suffer. How are you going to act if God lets you suffer?

67

Saul Meets Jesus

Jesus told his disciples that people would call them bad names. He said people would treat them badly. Look! Saul is calling the disciples bad names. He is treating them badly. But Saul is going to become a disciple, too. And he is going to suffer for the name of Jesus. Saul used to go to synagogues to find the Lord's disciples. He wanted to put them in prison. Now he is going to synagogues to make new disciples. He doesn't want to put them in prison anymore. He wants to free them from their sins. He is telling people that Jesus is the Son of God. He is telling everyone that Jesus is the Messiah!

In God's Words
Acts 9:1-22

[1]Saul was a man who wanted to bully and murder the Lord's disciples. Saul went to the high priest. [2]He asked the high priest to write letters to the synagogues in Damascus. Saul wanted permission to arrest any disciples he found in Damascus. He wanted to take these men and women to Jerusalem. [3]So he went off and came near to Damascus. Suddenly a light from heaven was shining all around him. [4]Saul fell to the ground. He heard a voice say to him, "Saul, Saul, why are you treating me badly?"

[5]Saul asked, "Who are you, Lord?"

He said, "I am Jesus. You are treating me badly. [6]Now get up and go into the city. Then you will be told what you have to do."

[7]Some men were on the road with Saul. They stood there and didn't say a word. They heard the voice but did not see anyone. [8]Saul

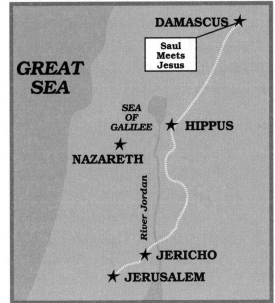

got up from the ground. He opened his eyes but he could not see anything. So they led him by the hand into Damascus. ⁹For three days Saul could not see. He did not eat a thing and he did not drink.

¹⁰A disciple named Ananias lived in Damascus. The Lord spoke to him in a vision, "Ananias!"

"Here I am, Lord!" he said.

¹¹The Lord said to him, "Get up and go to Straight Street. Go to the house of Judas. Ask for a man from Tarsus named Saul. Right now Saul is praying. ¹²He has seen a vision about a man named Ananias. Ananias came and put his hands on Saul. Then he could see again."

¹³Ananias said, "Lord, I have heard many things about this man. He has done all kinds of bad things to your holy people in Jerusalem. ¹⁴And here he has permission from the chief priests. He can arrest anyone who calls on your name."

¹⁵But the Lord said to Ananias, "Go! This man is my chosen servant. He will carry my name before the nations and their kings. He will carry my name before the people of Israel. ¹⁶I will show him how much he has to suffer for my name."

¹⁷So Ananias went to the house and went inside. He put his hands on Saul. He said, "Brother Saul, the Lord Jesus appeared to you on the road as you were coming here. The Lord sent me so that you could see again and be filled with the Holy Spirit." ¹⁸Right then something crusty fell from Saul's eyes. Saul could see again! He got up and was baptized. ¹⁹Saul ate some food and became strong again.

Saul stayed with the disciples in Damascus for many days. ²⁰Right away he went to the synagogues and taught about Jesus. He said, "This man is the Son of God!" ²¹Everyone who heard him was surprised. They said, "Isn't this the man who hurt people who called on the

name of Jesus in Jerusalem? Didn't he just come here to arrest such people? Didn't he want to take them to the chief priests?" ²²But Saul became stronger and stronger. He won arguments with the Jews who lived in Damascus. He proved that Jesus is the Messiah.

In Your Words

1. Jesus spoke to Saul on the road to Damascus. There were some men with him. Did they see Jesus? Did they hear anything?

2. Why were the people surprised when they heard Saul telling others about Jesus?

3. Saul was also known as Paul. He used to hurt the disciples. But he became a very important disciple. Look in the list of letters in the New Testament (page 198). How many of those books were written by Paul, the Lord's disciple?

68
Living Sacrifices

You have one body. Your body has many parts. But think what it would be like if your whole body was a nose! You'd be able to smell swell, but how could you eat anything. Imagine that your whole body was one big mouth. Then you could eat and you could talk. But you couldn't smell anything you were eating! Aren't you glad your body has many parts?

The **church** is like your body. It is one body. But it has many parts. Each person is a part of the church. Each person has a different job to do. One part isn't better than another part. Each part is just different.

In Other Words

church. A group of people who believe that Jesus died and lives to save them from their sins.

We can **encourage** people in different ways. Sometimes encouraging is telling people the right things to do. Sometimes it is helping sad people feel better.

prophecy. Remember the prophets in the Old Testament? They told God's word to the people. The gift of prophecy is telling God's word to people.

In God's Words
Romans 12:1-18

[1]God has shown us all his mercy. So I ask you to do this, my brothers and sisters. Offer your bodies to God as living sacrifices, holy and pleasing to God. This is the right way to serve God. [2]Do not act the way this world wants you to act. But act differently. Use

196

your mind in a new way. Then you will understand God's will. His will is good and pleasing and perfect.

[3]I speak to every one of you by the grace God gave to me. Do not think that you are more important than you really are. Think about yourself carefully. Judge yourself by the faith God has given you. [4]Each of us has one body with many parts. And these parts do not all do the same thing. [5]In the same way, we are many people. But in Christ we are one body. And each member belongs to all the others. [6]Each of us has different gifts by the grace God has given us. If your gift is prophecy, then use your faith to **prophesy**. [7]If your gift is serving others, then serve. If your gift is teaching, then teach. [8]If your gift is **encouraging**, then encourage. If your gift is sharing what you have with others, do it with all your heart. If your gift is leading, do your very best. If your gift is showing mercy, do it with happiness.

[9]Love must be real and true. Hate what is evil. Hold tight to what is good. [10]Love each other warmly with brotherly love. Treat others as more important than yourselves. [11]Always be ready to do your very best. Keep your spirit strong and alive. Serve the Lord. [12]Be joyful in hope. Be patient when you are treated badly. Pray all the time. [13]Share what you have with God's holy people who are in need. Take care of strangers.

[14]Bless those who treat you badly. Bless and do not curse. [15]Be happy with those who are happy. Cry with those who cry. [16]Get along with each other. Do not think you are better than everyone else. Be friends with people who are not important or popular. Do not think you know it all.

[17]If someone does evil to you, do not pay them back with evil. Be careful to do what everyone thinks is right. [18]If it can be done, if you are able, live at peace with everyone.

In Your Words

1. Paul teaches us how to get along with others. When someone is happy, what should we do? When someone is sad, what should we do?

197

2. Are you better than me? Am I better than you? What does Paul say? Who does he say is better?

3. Long ago, the Israelites made burnt offerings to show that they belonged to Yahweh. The burnt offerings showed that they wanted to do things to please him. What can you do that shows Yahweh you want to please him? You may want to look at reading 51 for some ideas. How can you be a living sacrifice?

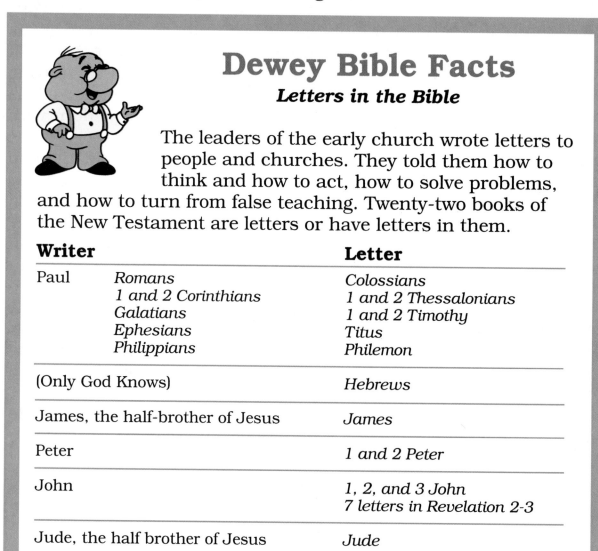

Dewey Bible Facts
Letters in the Bible

The leaders of the early church wrote letters to people and churches. They told them how to think and how to act, how to solve problems, and how to turn from false teaching. Twenty-two books of the New Testament are letters or have letters in them.

Writer		Letter
Paul	*Romans*	*Colossians*
	1 and 2 Corinthians	*1 and 2 Thessalonians*
	Galatians	*1 and 2 Timothy*
	Ephesians	*Titus*
	Philippians	*Philemon*
(Only God Knows)		*Hebrews*
James, the half-brother of Jesus		*James*
Peter		*1 and 2 Peter*
John		*1, 2, and 3 John*
		7 letters in Revelation 2-3
Jude, the half brother of Jesus		*Jude*

69

People of Faith

Do you hope that God will always be with you? Do you hope that one day you will live with God in heaven? Sometimes it's hard to keep hoping for these things. Since we can't see God with us, it's hard to believe that he is with us. Since we can't see heaven, it's hard to believe that heaven is real. But God has promised us these things. He wants us to be sure about his promises we do not see. He wants us to know that what we hope for is real. He wants us to believe what he has said. He wants us to have **faith**

In Other Words

Faith is not playing make-believe. Faith is not pretending. Faith is believing what God has said.

Righteousness is something we can do or a way we can be. It is doing right things or being right with God.

In God's Words
Hebrews 11:1-4,6-9,11-12

[1]Faith is knowing that what we hope for is real. Faith is being sure about things we do not see. [2]God said good things about people long ago because they had faith.

[3]By faith we know that all things were created by God's word. Before God made the things that we see, there was nothing to see!

[4]By faith Abel offered a better sacrifice to God than Cain did. By faith Abel showed he was a **righteous** man. God said good things about him. God said good things about Abel's offerings. And by faith Abel still speaks today, even though he is dead.

[6]Without faith no one can please God. Anyone who comes to God must believe that God is real and that God rewards people who look for him.

[7]By faith Noah heard a warning from God about things he could not see. By faith Noah built a boat and saved his family. By faith

Noah showed that the world was wrong. Noah received the **righteousness** that comes from faith.

⁸By faith Abraham obeyed when God called him. He went to a place that God was about to give him. Abraham went even though he did not know were he was going. ⁹By faith he stayed as a stranger in the land God promised him. He lived in tents. So did Isaac and Jacob. God also promised them that they would receive the land.

¹¹By faith Abraham received the power to become a father. (Abraham was way too old to become a father and Sarah could not have children.) Abraham believed that God was faithful to do what he had promised. ¹²Abraham was as good as dead. But through this one man came many descendants. They were as many as the stars in the sky. Like the sand on the seashore, you could not count them all!

In Your Words

1. What did Noah do when he heard God's warning about things he could not see?

2. What did Abraham do when God told him to go to a new land?

3. Abel, Noah, and Abraham were amazing people. They believed what God had said. They believed his promises. You can be an amazing person, too. How will you be an amazing child for God?

70
The Second Letter of the Elder John

Have you ever met a little boy who says he knows how to do something? But you know he doesn't. Maybe he told you he knows how to somersault off the high dive at the swimming pool. If he was going to teach you how to somersault off the high dive, I would warn you not to let him teach you. He's pretending. Don't learn from him. Maybe he can't even swim!

The elder John is warning a lady about false teachers. He is warning her about teachers who pretend to know God. But they don't really know him. Just as you wouldn't want to learn diving from a pretend teacher, don't learn about Jesus from a pretend teacher either. John is warning the lady. Listen to his warning, too.

In Other Words

An **antichrist** is a pretend christ. He is someone who says he is the Messiah, the Son of God. But only Jesus is the Son of God. Only Jesus is the Messiah.

John writes to the lady whom God has **chosen**. That means she is a Christian.

Children are people in the lady's church. They are probably the people she told about Jesus. They are the people who believed in Jesus when she told them about him.

The apostle John calls himself "the **elder**." This means two things. It means he was an older man and a man with authority. He was a man people had to obey.

201

In God's Words
2 John

¹From the **elder**:

To the lady God has **chosen** and to her **children**. I love them in the truth. (I am not the only one who loves her children. Everyone who knows the truth loves them, too.) ²I am writing because of the truth. The truth lives in us and will be with us forever.

³Grace, mercy, and peace will be with us in truth and love. Grace, mercy, and peace come from God the Father and from Jesus Christ, the Father's Son.

⁴I was very happy to find some of your children walking in the truth. This is what the Father commanded us. ⁵Dear lady, I am not writing you a new command. I am writing the command we have had from the beginning. I ask that we love each other. ⁶And this is love: that we walk in obedience to God's commands. This is what you have heard from the beginning. God's command is that you walk in love.

⁷Many liars have gone out into the world. They do not believe that Jesus Christ came to earth as a human being. This kind of person is the liar and the **antichrist**.

⁸Be careful that you do not lose what you have worked for! Watch out so that you may get your full reward! ⁹Anyone who goes their own way, anyone who does not continue to believe the teaching about Christ, does not have God. But anyone who continues to believe the teaching has both the Father and the Son.

¹⁰Someone might come to you who does not bring the right teaching about Jesus. Do not take him into your house. Do not even welcome him. ¹¹Anyone who welcomes him actually helps him with his wicked work!

¹²I have much to write to you, but I do not want to write with paper and ink. I would rather visit you and talk with you face to face. Then we will be happy together!

¹³The children of your chosen sister send their greetings.

In Your Words

1. What is the command John is writing to the lady?

2. What does an antichrist tell people?

3. How can you love your mom and dad, your brother or sister, your friend down the street? Choose one thing you will do today or tommorrow to show love to someone close to you.

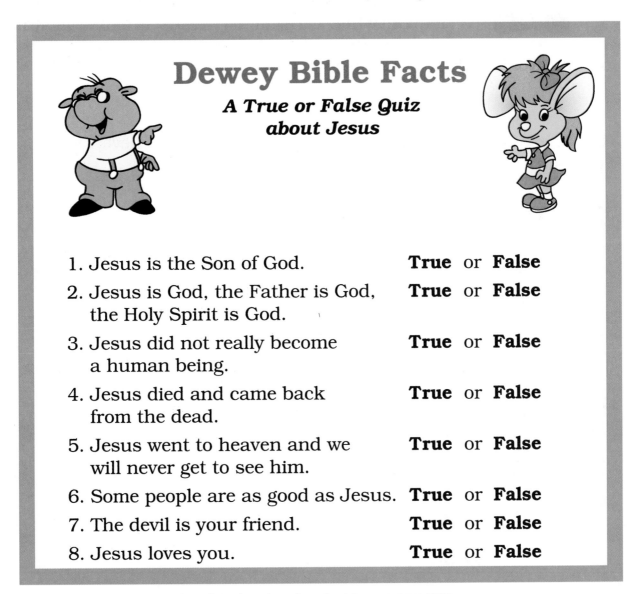

Dewey Bible Facts

A True or False Quiz about Jesus

1. Jesus is the Son of God.   **True** or **False**

2. Jesus is God, the Father is God,   **True** or **False**
   the Holy Spirit is God.

3. Jesus did not really become   **True** or **False**
   a human being.

4. Jesus died and came back   **True** or **False**
   from the dead.

5. Jesus went to heaven and we   **True** or **False**
   will never get to see him.

6. Some people are as good as Jesus. **True** or **False**

7. The devil is your friend.   **True** or **False**

8. Jesus loves you.   **True** or **False**

ANSWERS: 1.T, 2.T, 3.F, 4.T, 5.F, 6.F, 7.F, 8.T

71

Jesus Speaks to His Church

Revelation is a book like Daniel. It tells us about the future in strange and wonderful ways. Some parts are hard to understand. Other parts are easy to understand. Four things are easy to understand. First, Jesus is coming again. Second, people who believe in Jesus will live with him forever. Third, people who did not believe in Jesus will be punished forever. And fourth, while we wait for Jesus to come again, we need to live by faith. We need to live by faith just like Noah and Abraham lived by faith.

In Other Words

The **Amen** is a name for Jesus. It means you can believe him. His word is true.

A **revelation** shows something that was hidden. Jesus sent an angel to show John things no one else could see. He told John things about the future that no one else knew. Jesus gave John a revelation.

Overcoming is winning the fight against evil. Jesus was tempted not to do the Father's will. But he overcame. He died on the cross for our sins. He wants us to overcome, too.

In God's Words

Revelation 1:1-3

[1]The **revelation** of Jesus Christ. God gave Jesus this revelation to show his servants things that would happen very soon. Jesus sent his angel to tell his servant John. [2]John is a witness to everything he saw. He is a witness to the word of God and the witness of Jesus Christ. [3]Everyone who reads the words of this prophecy is blessed. Those who hear the words and do what is written are also blessed. The time is near!

Revelation 3:14-22

[14]"Write this to the angel of the church in Laodicea:

These are the words of the **Amen**. I am the witness you can believe. My witness is true. All God's creation came from me. [15]I know what you do. I know that you are not cold and you are not

hot. I wish you were cold or hot! [16]You are neither hot nor cold—you are lukewarm. So I am going to spit you out of my mouth! [17]You say, 'I am rich. I am rich and I don't need a thing.' But you do not know how needy you are! You need mercy. You are poor and blind and naked. [18]I tell you: Buy gold from me. I have gold that was made pure in the fire. Then you will be rich. Buy white clothes to wear. Then you can cover your nakedness and not be embarrassed. Buy medicine to put on your eyes. Then you will see.

[19]I warn and discipline those whom I love. So do your best! Repent. [20]Listen! I am standing at the door. I am knocking. If you hear my voice and open the door, I will come in. I will eat with you, and you with me.

[21]If you **overcome**, I will let you sit with me on my throne. That is what I did. I overcame and sat down with my Father on his throne. [22]If you have an ear, listen to what the Spirit says to the churches."

In Your Words

1. God blesses people who make peace. God blesses people who are treated badly because they do right. In this reading, God blesses people too. What do they need to do for God to bless them?

2. Jesus is strong. He overcame and sat down with his Father on his throne. Jesus wants us to overcome, too. We aren't as strong as Jesus. How can we overcome?

3. Jesus asked the church in Laodicea to buy gold and clothes and medicine from him. He meant the riches they had on earth were not riches in heaven. What are some things you can do now that will make you rich in heaven?

72
Jesus Is Coming Soon

In the beginning, God made the heavens and the earth. He made a beautiful garden. He put Adam in the garden. John saw the new heaven and the new earth God will make one day. The angel showed it to him. It will have a beautiful garden, too. Read the facts Dewey's collected for you about the Garden of Eden and the Garden of Revelation. We can't go back to the Garden of Eden. But one day we'll be able to go to the Garden of Revelation.

In Other Words

In Revelation, Jesus is often called the **Lamb**. Jesus is our Passover Lamb. He died for our sins so that we could live forever. God wants us to remember that always.

In God's Words
Revelation 21:1-5

[1]I saw a new heaven and a new earth. The first heaven and the first earth had gone away. There was no more sea. [2]I saw the Holy City, the new Jerusalem. The city was coming down out of heaven from God. It was made up like a bride all dressed up for her

husband. ³I heard a loud voice from the throne. It said, "Now the place where God lives is with people. He will live with them. They will be his people. God himself will be with them. He will be their God. ⁴He will wipe every tear from their eyes. There will be no more death. There will be no more sadness or crying or pain. The way things used to be has gone away."

⁵The one sitting on the throne said, "Look! I am making everything new!" Then he said, "Write this down. These words you can believe. They are true."

Revelation 22:1-7

¹Then the angel showed me the river of the water of life. The river was as clear as glass. It was flowing from the throne of God and of the **Lamb**. ²It flowed down the middle of the wide street in the city. On each side of the river stood the tree of life. The tree has twelve kinds of fruit. It has fruit every month. The leaves of the tree are for healing the nations. ³There will be no more curse. The throne of God and of the Lamb will be in the city. God's servants will serve him. ⁴They will see his face. God's name will be on their foreheads. ⁵There will be no more night. People will not need light from a lamp or light from the sun. The Lord God will give them light. And they will rule for ever and ever.

⁶The angel said to me, "These words you can believe. They are true. The Lord is the God of the spirits of the prophets. The Lord sent his angel to show his servants the things that must happen very soon."

⁷"Listen! I am coming soon! Everyone who obeys the words of the prophecy in this book is blessed."

In Your Words

1. People will live in the new Jerusalem. Who else will live with the people in the new Jerusalem?

2. After Adam and Eve sinned, Yahweh God put angels in the

Garden of Eden. He put them in the garden to guard the way to the tree of life. Do you see angels guarding the tree of life in the Garden of Revelation? Why do you think they aren't guarding the way to the tree of life anymore?

3. One day, God's servants will serve him in the new Jerusalem. But you and I can serve God today! John heard Jesus say, "Listen! I am coming soon!" He is coming soon. What can you do to be ready for him when he comes?

Dewey Bible Facts

The First Heaven and Earth	The New Heaven and Earth
Darkness covered the earth.	No more night.
The sea covered the earth.	No more sea.
Light came from sun, moon, and stars.	It is always light because of the glory of God and the glory of the Lamb.
God sometimes walked with his people.	God always lives with his people.
People, animals, and the earth were cursed because of sin.	No more curse.
People suffered and cried and died because of sin.	No more death or sadness. No more crying or pain.

Glossary

adultery (see reading 24). Adultery is having sexual relations with someone else's husband or wife. God says adultery is wrong.

altar (see reading 10). A pile of stones. People made their offerings to God on an altar.

Amen (see reading 71). The Amen is a name for Jesus. It means he is faithful and true.

angels (see reading 48). Angels are special servants of God. Sometimes God sends angels from heaven with special messages for his people. Angels look like people but they are not people.

anoint (see reading 33). Samuel anointed both Saul and David. That means he poured olive oil on their heads. The anointing showed the people that the Holy Spirit was coming to make the person strong and successful.

anoint his head with oil (see reading 36). In Bible times, if a special guest came to your house for dinner you would anoint his head with oil and wash his feet.

antichrist (see reading 70). An antichrist is a pretend christ. He is someone who says he is the Messiah, the Son of God. But only Jesus is the Son of God. Only Jesus is the Messiah.

apostles (see reading 60). Jesus chose twelve apostles to learn about him. Then he sent them to tell the whole world about Jesus, the Holy Spirit, and the kingdom of God.

appear (see reading 1). Now you can see it. Before you could not. It appeared!

Aramaic, Latin, and Greek (see reading 63). Aramaic, Latin, and Greek were different languages spoken in Israel. Aramaic was the language of the Jewish people. Latin was the language of the Roman rulers and soldiers. Greek was the language that both Jewish people and Roman people understood.

ark of God (see reading 37). The ark of God was a wooden box covered with gold. It had two gold angels on its top. It was a model on earth of God's throne in heaven. Sometimes it is called the ark of the covenant.

authority (see reading 64). A person with authority is powerful. He can control many things. Jesus obeyed the authority of God his Father. Now the Father has given Jesus authority over all things. We need to obey Jesus' authority as he obeyed his Father's authority.

Baal and **Ashtoreth** (see reading 31). Baal and Ashtoreth were two favorite make-believe gods of the Canaanites. Their ways were evil. The people thought they were mean gods.

baptized (see reading 50). John baptized people by carefully dunking them in the Jordan River. To be baptized showed that people were different. It showed that they were part of John's group. Even Jesus was baptized. He wanted to show others that he was part of this new group of people who pleased God.

because of his Name (see reading 36). God's name is Yahweh. Yahweh means God is with us to save us and to help us. Yahweh saves us and helps us because of who he is, because of his Name.

betrayed (see reading 62). Judas was a member of Jesus' group. But Judas told Jesus' enemies where they could find Jesus. He betrayed Jesus. Judas was a traitor.

bless (see reading 2). God's blessing is his promise to do something good. He always makes his promises happen.

bronze (see reading 47). A shiny metal. Bronze is a yellow-brown color.

burnt offerings (see reading 25). Israelites made burnt offerings to show that they belonged to Yahweh and that they wanted to do things to please him.

call on the name of Yahweh (see reading 7). Talking to the right God; praying to God by name.

caravan (see reading 14). In Bible times, traders had to travel in caravans, going from place to place with their packages. Some people made their living going from place to place buying things and selling things.

chosen (see reading 70). John writes to the lady whom God has chosen. That means she is a Christian.

Christ (see reading 50). Christ is Jesus' title. It means "anointed one." Just like Samuel anointed David to be the king of Israel, God anointed Jesus to be the king of the world. "Christ" is the same as the word "Messiah."

church (see reading 68). The church is a group of people who believe that Jesus died and lives to save them from their sin.

cistern (see reading 14). A cistern is a large pit for catching rain water.

clean animals and **clean birds** (see reading 10). These are animals God wanted to be given back to him as offerings.

cloaks (see reading 58). Cloaks are like coats. People wore cloaks when the weather was cool. John the Baptist had a cloak made from camel's hair.

command/commandment (see reading 24). A commandment is something good God wants you to do or something bad God doesn't want you to do.

compassionate and **gracious** (see reading 26). God is compassionate when he does good things for people who need help. He is gracious when he does good things for people who don't deserve his help.

concern (see reading 18). When someone is concerned, he cares. Sometimes the people of Israel feel like God doesn't care when they hurt. He always knows what's happening to them. But God does care. He is always ready to help them.

covenant (see reading 8). If you do something for me, I'll do something for you. Let's write down our promises so we won't forget them. And let's have some other people hear us make our promises to each other. That's a covenant.

covet (see reading 24). If you want something bad enough to steal it, that is coveting.

cross (see reading 63). In the time of Jesus, the worst criminals were crucified. They were tied or nailed to a wooden cross, shaped like a "T" or a "+."

crucify (see reading 63). In the time of Jesus, the worst criminals were crucified. They were tied or nailed to a wooden cross until they died. Jesus loved us so much, he died for us on a cross. He died on a cross just like the worst criminals.

curse (see reading 6). When God blesses, he promises to do something good. When God curses, he promises to punish evil or sin.

Glossary

Daughter Zion (see reading 58). Zion is a name for the city of Jerusalem, God's favorite city where his temple was built. He calls Zion his daughter because the city is so important to him.

descendant (see reading 12). You are a descendant of your parents. That means you came from them. You are a descendant of your grandparents. You are even a descendant of Adam and Eve.

disciples (see reading 51). Disciples are people who follow Jesus—like Peter and James in the New Testament, and like you and me today!

discipline (see reading 41). When we're taught how to do things God's way, that's discipline. When we're punished for not doing what we're taught, that's discipline, too.

dream (see reading 13). In the Bible God used dreams to tell special people about secret things he wanted them to know. The most famous people who had these types of dreams were called prophets.

elder (see reading 70). The apostle John calls himself "the elder." This means two things. It means he was an older man and a man with authority. He was a man people had to obey.

empty (see reading 1). Nothing on the earth was like we see it today. There were no apples and no caterpillars. The only thing on the earth was water.

encouraging (see reading 68). There are different ways of encouraging people. Sometimes encouraging is telling people the right things to do. Sometimes it is helping sad people feel better.

Eternal Father (see reading 45). A king should be like a father to his people. This king is a father who lives forever.

eternal life (see reading 53). People who believe in Jesus enter the kingdom of God. They are "born again." They live forever.

evil one (see reading 52). The evil one is Satan, the devil. He wants to tempt us to sin against God.

faith (see reading 69). Faith is not pretending. Faith is believing what God has said.

famine (see reading 56). A famine is when there is no food to eat.

Father (see reading 49). When Jesus talks about his Father, he is talking about God, not Joseph.

Father, Son, and Holy Spirit (see reading 64). God is one. That's why he has one name. But God is three. The Father, the Son, and the Holy Spirit are God. This is a "mystery" even grown-ups cannot understand. We refer to God as the "Trinity." This means God is three in one.

fear God (see reading 12). When bad people fear God, they are afraid of him. When good people fear God, they respect him, they love him, and they obey him.

Feast of Passover (see reading 49). This is one of three feasts the Jews came to Jerusalem to celebrate each year. It helped them remember the strong way God freed them from their slavery in Egypt.

fellowship offerings (see reading 25). Fellowship offerings were like having a special dinner with God—just you and him!

firstborn (see reading 21). The child born first in any family is special. Israel is God's firstborn. They are the first people God chose to be his special nation.

forgive (see reading 16). If someone does something to hurt you, you can get even, pay him back, or hurt him Or you can forgive him. That means you won't get even, or pay him back, or hurt him.

forgiving (see reading 26). When people repent from their sins God forgives them. He doesn't punish them.

from Dan to Beersheba (see reading 32). The city of Dan is at the "top" of Israel in the north. Beersheba is at the "bottom," in the south. "From Dan to Beersheba" means the whole land and all the people of Israel.

full of love and faithfulness (see reading 26). God is always there to do good for those who love and obey him.

gave up his own spirit (see reading 63). Jesus loved us so much, he died for us on a cross. He died on a cross just like the worst criminals. He died because he wanted to. No one made him die—he gave up his own spirit.

generation (see reading 31). A generation is made up of people who are about the same age. The other children in your school are in your generation. Your teachers are in your parents' generation.

glory/the glory of God (see readings 29, 48). Glory is something we can see that tells us what God is like and what he does. Before God made the sun, moon, and stars there was light. That shiny light was probably God's glory. In the new Jerusalem there won't be a sun, a moon, or stars. Jesus will be the city's lamp! His glory will light up the city.

God changes his mind (see reading 25). God doesn't change his mind like we do. When he changes his mind, it means he changes his actions because people have changed their actions.

God knows (see reading 12). Sometimes God says he now knows something. He doesn't mean he has just learned something new. God knows everything. When God says he now knows something he means he has experienced something with us.

God remembers (see reading 9). When you remember something, it means you forgot it first. When God remembers something, he's doing what he once promised to do. God never forgets his promises.

God's book of life (see reading 47). People who love and obey God have their names written in God's book of life.

good and evil (see reading 4). Good is doing what God wants. Not doing what God wants you to do is evil.

government (see reading 45). People who are in charge of other people. People who make rules for others to follow.

heart (see reading 33). Yahweh knows what we are thinking and feeling. He even knows why we choose to do the things we do. He can look at our heart, where we think and feel and choose.

Hebrew (see reading 17). A Hebrew is another word for Israelite.

high priest (see reading 62). Priests led the Israelites in their worship of God. The high priest was the leader of the priests. He was a very important leader in Israel.

holy (see reading 3). Holy means different. But it is different God's way. God worked for six days. God rested on the seventh day. The seventh day is different. That is why the seventh day is holy.

213

Glossary

holy place (see reading 22). Remember holy means "different." But it is different God's way. A holy place is a different place used to worship God.

hosanna (see reading 58). Hosanna is a Hebrew word. It means "Save us, please!"

humility (see reading 41). Humility is not thinking you're better than everybody else. When you think you're better than everybody else, that's pride. God likes humility. But he hates pride.

hyssop (see reading 38). Hyssop is a plant the Israelites used like a brush.

I AM (see reading 62). God told Moses that his name was I AM. Jesus also told the people that his name is I AM. Both God the Father and Jesus are I AM.

idols (see reading 24). Idols are make-believe gods. Some people make things out of wood or metal and say that they are gods. Only Yahweh is God.

image (see reading 3). God made people in his image. That doesn't mean we look like God or are as strong as God. And it doesn't mean we are little gods. It means we can talk and think and act like God does.

incense (see reading 44). Incense was burned like an offering to God or an offering to the make-believe gods. It smelled good.

Israel and Judah (see reading 44). After King Solomon died, the Israelites were split into two kingdoms. The northern kingdom was called Israel. The southern kingdom was called Judah. Neither kingdom loved and obeyed Yahweh. So Yahweh punished them and sent them out of the pleasant land.

Israelite (see reading 17). Children of Israel are Israelites. They are the descendants of Jacob.

Jacob/Israel (see reading 14). Names are important to God. God changed Jacob's name to Israel. The name "Israel" means "he struggles with God."

kinds (see reading 2). Dogs have puppies and cats have kittens. People, animals, and plants always have babies that are like them.

kingdom (see reading 37). The place where people obey the king is the kingdom. A kingdom lasts only as long as the king is strong enough to defeat those who want to take the kingdom.

Lamb (see reading 72). In Revelation, Jesus is often called the Lamb. Jesus is our Passover Lamb. He died for our sins so that we could live forever.

lame (see reading 58). A lame person cannot walk. Jesus made the lame walk. He made the blind see.

Law and the Prophets (see reading 59). The Law and the Prophets were the two largest parts of the Jewish Bible. Christians call these books the Old Testament.

Levi/Levite (see reading 18). Levi was one of the twelve sons of Jacob. Moses and his brother were Levites. They would one day help God's people worship God in the right way.

locust (see reading 21). A locust is a large grasshopper.

manger (see reading 48). A manger is a feeding box for animals. You slept in a crib when you were a baby. Jesus slept in a manger!

meditate (see reading 30). When we meditate, we talk to ourself about what God is like and what he has done. When we tell others what God is like and what he has done, that's praise.

medium (see reading 35). Someone who worshiped the pretend gods. They thought they could talk to ghosts. Saul went to a medium to see what the ghost of Samuel would tell him to do. It was a bad thing to do.

mercy (see readings 25, 51). People who show mercy are good and kind to people who are hurting or in trouble.

Messiah (see readings 48, 59). Messiah means "anointed." The Jewish people were waiting for God to send the Messiah to save them from their enemies. They did not understand that God wanted the Messiah to save them from their sins. They did not understand that Jesus was the Messiah, the Christ, the son of David, the son of God.

midwife (see reading 17). A woman whose job is to help mothers give birth to their babies.

Mighty God (see reading 45). A king should be mighty. He should be strong. This king is not only mighty. He is God!

Miracle (see Signs and Miracles).

mourn (see reading 51). People who mourn are people who are sad that they sin against God. They are sad that other people sin against God too. They ask God to forgive them.

murder (see reading 24). If a person kills another person just because he wants to, that is murder. In the Bible, God sometimes commanded his people to kill other people in war. God sometimes commanded his people to kill other

people as punishment for their sin. This is not murder.

name (see reading 37). To have a great name means to be famous. It means to be famous for good things.

new covenant (see reading 60). God made a covenant with Israel at Mount Sinai. The Ten Commandments were part of that covenant (reading 24). Israel promised to do everything that God told them, but they did not obey God. They broke the covenant. So God made a new covenant with all people. He sent his son Jesus to die for our sins and to come back to life again. If you believe in Jesus you have eternal life. You are part of God's new covenant.

offering (see reading 7). God owns the whole world, but he still wants us to give some of it back to him. In Bible days, people gave back to God the best of what they worked for.

order (see reading 1). When things have order, they are in the right place. And they work just right. God put all things on the earth in the right place and made them work just right.

overcome (see reading 71). Overcoming is winning the fight against evil. Jesus was tempted not to do the Father's will. But he overcame. He died on the cross for our sins. He wants us to overcome too.

papyrus (see reading 18). A plant that grows in the water. It was used to make baskets and sheets of paper.

Pharaoh (see reading 17). The special name for the king of Egypt.

Pharisees (see reading 59). Pharisees were leaders of the Jewish people. The people thought the Pharisees were very important and godly people. But Jesus

Glossary

said that the Pharisees wanted to please people more than they wanted to please God. The Pharisees did not like Jesus.

poor in spirit (see reading 51). People who know that they have nothing to offer God are poor in spirit. They know they are helpless without God.

praise (see reading 39). Praise is telling others what God is like and what he has done.

pregnant (see reading 7). When a woman has a baby growing inside her, she is pregnant.

priest (see reading 19). A man who leads people in their worship of God. He prays for them. He blesses them. And he makes offerings for them.

Prince of Peace (see reading 45). A king should try to give peace to his people. This king will give peace to people he is pleased with.

prophecy (see reading 68). The gift of prophecy is telling God's word to people.

prophets and seers (see reading 44). Prophets and seers are men and women God spoke to just like he spoke to Moses and Samuel. They often told the people to quit doing bad things, and to love and obey God instead.

proverbs (see reading 41). Proverbs are short poems or sayings. They help us know how to live the way God wants us to live.

pure in heart (see reading 51). People who are pure in heart don't try to lie to God. They love God more than anything!

ram's horn (see reading 33). Some ram's horns were used like trumpets to call the people to worship. Other ram's horns were used like bottles.

repent (see readings 26, 65). We repent when we stop doing wrong and then ask God to forgive us.

rest (see reading 3). When we are tired we go to sleep. That's not how God rests. When he rests he's not making any new things.

resurrection (see reading 65). Resurrection means rising from the dead. God raised Jesus from the dead. Everyone who believes in Jesus will also be raised from the dead.

reveal, revelation (see reading 32). We cannot see God. We only know what he is like and what he wants us to do if he reveals himself to us. God has revealed himself in the things he did for Israel. God has revealed himself in the words he spoke to the prophets. God's greatest revelation is in the life and words of his Son Jesus. We have God's revelation in the Bible.

revelation (see reading 71). A revelation shows something that was hidden. Jesus sent an angel to show John things no one else could see. He told John things about the future that no one else knew. Jesus gave John a revelation.

righteous (see reading 8). People who are righteous do what is right. They choose to do what God wants them to do.

righteousness (see reading 69). Righteousness is something we can do or a way we can be. It is doing right things or being right with God.

rule (see reading 3). God wants people to take good care of his world. And he doesn't want anyone to harm his animals just for fun.

Sabbath day (see reading 24). This is the seventh day. When God made the world, he rested on the seventh (Sabbath) day. This made it holy.

sackcloth (see reading 14). Sackcloth is rough, scratchy cloth that people would wear when they were very sad. When they were crying for someone in their family who died they would wear sackcloth.

sacrifice (see reading 33). An offering that involves the killing of an animal.

Sadducees (see reading 66). The Sadducees were an important group of Jewish leaders. They did not believe in miracles or in angels or in the resurrection. But God showed the Sadducees that all these things were true!

sexual relations (see reading 7). What a husband and wife who love each other do together to make babies.

shepherd's rod (see reading 36). This is a large, heavy club shepherds used to fight off lions and bears and wolves. A shepherd used his rod to protect his sheep.

shepherd's staff (see reading 36). This was a stick shepherds used to guide their sheep. A shepherd used his staff to keep his sheep from wandering away and getting lost.

signs and **miracles** (see readings 20, 55, 66). God does signs and miracles for people. He wants to show us that a person who says he is from God is really from God. Signs and miracles are unusual. They don't work the way things usually work.

simple people (see reading 29). Simple people are people who still have a lot to learn. They have not yet decided to be good or bad. All of you young readers are "simple." You become wise when you choose to follow God's ways as you learn about him.

sin (see reading 5). Sin is doing something evil. It is doing something God doesn't want you to do.

slavery (see reading 17). Slavery is not like having a job. It's life or death. If you work for your master you live. If you don't work for your master you die.

sling (see reading 34). A sling was a long strip of leather with a pocket in the middle. The pocket held a rock. A person swung the sling like a propeller and then let go of one of the ends. The rock then sailed through the air. Golf-ball size rocks traveled up to one hundred yards.

slow to anger (see reading 26). God doesn't punish us as soon as we sin. He wants to give us time to repent. If we repent, then he doesn't have to punish us.

smart, wise, and **know** (see reading 5). These three words have similar meaning. When good people are smart, they do good things. When evil people are smart, they often do bad things. Smart people know a lot of things. When smart people do good things, that makes them wise.

Son of Man (see reading 60). Son of Man means "human being." It also is a special, secret name for the Messiah. Jesus liked to call himself the Son of Man. His disciples knew that meant he was the Messiah.

spirit came back (see reading 54). When people die, their body stays on earth but their spirit goes to God. When Jesus raised Jairus' daughter from the dead, her spirit came back into her body. She was alive again!

successful (see reading 30). When you do something God wants you to do, you are successful.

Glossary

synagogue (see reading 54). A synagogue is a building where Jewish people meet to study the Bible and pray to God. It is like a Jewish church.

tax collectors (see reading 57). Tax collectors collected money that people had to pay to the leaders of their country. Sometimes the tax collectors made the people pay *more* money than they had to! That is why some tax collectors were rich. That is why people hated tax collectors and called them sinful.

teachers (see reading 49). These men knew all about the Bible. They would help people understand what the Bible said. Today people go to court when they can't solve a problem with another person. In Bible times, the people went to the teachers. The teachers helped them solve their problems with each other.

temple (see reading 49). The temple was God's house. It was a special place where God showed his glory.

this cup (see reading 61). The cup of wine at the Passover dinner was a picture for Jesus' blood. When Jesus died for us, blood came from his wounds. This cup also pictures his death. Jesus did not want to die; he did not want to "drink this cup." But he chose to do what God the Father wanted.

tomb (see reading 64). A tomb is a place where someone's body is put after he dies. Jesus' tomb was a cave dug out of solid rock. A round stone—like a wheel—was rolled over the opening of the tomb. It could be rolled away to put other bodies in. But an angel rolled the stone away from Jesus' tomb to show that Jesus' body was not there any more!

treat his name as holy (see reading 52). God's name is holy. When people obey him, and pray to him, and praise him, they treat his name as holy.

treat the name of God badly (see reading 24, question 3). If you use God's name to swear at someone, you are using it badly. If you "promise to God" to do something, but you do not do it, you are using his name badly. We should only use God's name when we talk about God and when we sing and pray to him. That is using God's name well.

uncircumcised Philistine (see reading 34). The Philistines lived between the Israelites and the sea. They were called uncircumcised because they didn't have a covenant with God like the Israelites did.

unfaithful (see reading 35). When you are faithful, you obey God. When you are unfaithful, you disobey God.

violence (see reading 8). When there is violence, people are hurting each other. They are attacking each other.

vision (see reading 47). A message God tells a prophet when the prophet is awake.

warrior (see reading 22). Someone who fights in wars. A soldier.

will is done (see reading 52). When we obey God, then his will is done.

wisdom (see reading 40). Wisdom is knowing what is right and doing what is right. When people are wise, they are successful.

witnesses (see reading 65). Witnesses are people who see something happen. Peter and the other apostles saw Jesus after his resurrection. They told people what they saw. We are Jesus' witnesses too. We can tell people about Jesus.

Wonderful Counselor (see reading 45). A king should be a counselor. He should listen to his people and help them live wisely. But this king is a counselor who is wonderful. He makes us wonder at the things he says and does.

worship (see reading 12). When we worship God, we do things that show that we know he is God. We pray to him. We sing to him. We give him our offerings. We are happy that he is our God.

written in God's book (see reading 47). People who love and obey God have their names written in God's book of life.

Yahweh (see readings 4,19). Yahweh is God's special name. God explains that "Yahweh" means "I am who I am." It is a name no one else has. It is a name God gave to himself. His name tells us that he is a God who is always with us and who saves us. He wants to be remembered by this name always.

P.S. Don't forget to turn to page 225 to see the entire line of **The Amazing Bible Series**. Videos, musical cassettes and more! Plus a coupon that will save you money on any item in the series.

P.P.S. Enter the **Amazing Book Coloring Contest**, see page 227 for details.

THE AMAZING BIBLE
Series

- **THE AMAZING BIBLE** series mixes music and animation to bring the exciting world of the Bible to life. You'll learn along with Revver, Rikki, Dewey, Doc, and Franklin about real-life heroes, heart-throbbing dramas, fascinating facts and awe-inspiring wonders of the Good Book.

  - In *The Amazing Book* video, you'll discover interesting facts about the Bible and how God sent His Son to earth. A coloring book is also available.

  - In *The Amazing Children* video, you'll learn how important children are to God's plan. The audio cassette contains songs from the video plus many more. An activity book is also available.

  - In *The Amazing Miracles* video, you'll enjoy the antics of Revver and Rikki as they realize how God performed miracles in the past and how He still performs them today! The audio cassette contains songs from the video plus many more.